BEST-EVER GAMES

FOR YOUTH MINISTRY

LES CHRISTIE
THE GAME GUY

Gr☺up

Loveland, Colorado
www.group.com

D1041069

Group resources actually work!

This Group resource incorporates our R.E.A.L. approach to ministry. It reinforces a growing friendship with Jesus, encourages long-term learning, and results in life transformation, because it's

Relational
Learner-to-learner interaction enhances learning and builds Christian friendships.

Experiential
What learners experience through discussion and action sticks with them up to 9 times longer than what they simply hear or read.

Applicable
The aim of Christian education is to equip learners to be both hearers and doers of God's Word.

Learner-based
Learners understand and retain more when the learning process takes into consideration how they learn best.

BEST-EVER GAMES FOR YOUTH MINISTRY

Visit our website: **group.com**

Credits
Editor: Kate S. Holburn
Acquisitions Editor: Kelli B. Trujillo
Creative Development Editor: Mikal Keefer
Chief Creative Officer: Joani Schultz
Copy Editor: Victoria Boone
Art Director: Kari K. Monson
Print Production Artist: Joyce Douglas
Cover Art Director: Jeff A. Storm
Cover Designer: Ray Tollison Design
Cover Illustrator: Gary Locke
Illustrators: Gary Locke and Warner McGee
Production Manager: Dodie Tipton

Library of Congress Cataloging-in-Publication Data
Christie, Les John.
    Best-ever games for youth ministry / by Les Christie.
       p. cm.
    Includes index.
    ISBN 0-7644-2770-9 (pbk. : alk. paper)
    1. Church group work with youth. 2. Games in Christian education.
    I. Title.
    BV4447.C4775 2005
    259'.23--dc22
                                   2005003168

21 20 19 18   18 17 16 15 14
Printed in the United States of America.

ACKNOWLEDGMENTS

I am so thankful for my students, colleagues, and friends I have met around the world who have contributed in some way to this book: Shaun Almond, Dave Ambrose, Matt Augee, Sarah Bacon, Glenn Bannerman, Kevin Batangan, Mike Bates, Tomas Bayou, Jeff Bisht, Chuck Bomar, Josh Bravo, Mark Bridgeman, Matt Bromiley, Edmund Brooks, Russ Cantu, Marc Cardenas, Jacqueline Carey, Jaroy Carpenter, Josh Christian, Chap Clark, Dale Cobb, Amber Conrad, Jack Crabtree, Matt Crane, Emily Darlington, Rick Eweles, John Delke, Joshua Eduki, Heather Engstrom, Mark Helsel, Bill Faulconer, Heather Files, Kevin Forbes, Mike Forsstrom, Aaron Friesen, Frank Galey, Courtney Geyer, Kimi Gibson, Laurel Hall, Nick Hart, Katrice Hernandez, Lisa Hulphers, Justin Humphreys, Megan Hutchinson, Gina Inhelder, Zach Imboden, Josh Jarrett, Dan Jessup, Don Joel, Jeromy Johnson, Steve Jones, Jee Taek Joo, Chris Kambish, Lisa Karpan, David Kawaye, Gale Kelsy, Adrain Kesler, Choong Man Kim, Ben Kreeger, Lisa Lamb, Gavin Larson, Benjamin Lee, Jeremiah Lester, Rick Lawrence, Leo Lew, Greg Lewis, Cory Linstrum, Tic Long, John Losey, Harley Ludwig, Dennis Lucero, Fred Lynch, Jason Ma, Lisa Macedo, Benji MacNaughton, Rose Maddox, Daniel Marsden, Jim Matteri, Billy Maus, Jonathan McKee, Michelle Mayfield, Eric Meyers, Nathan Milenewicz-Olson, Carlos Miras, Fritz Moga, Jae Moore, Adrian Moreno, Brock Morgan, Adilson Muandumba, Richelle Murray, Diane Nance, Devin Nelson, Mark Oestreicher, Eddie Passmore, Marv Penner, Ed Perez, Jared Pimentel, Laurie Polich, Don Porter, Brad Prather, Peter Pun, Sarah Quintana, William Race, Chris Reed, Wayne Rice, Duffy Robbins, Sabrina Rosch, Joe Ryan, Emilie Sampson, Matt Sampson, Chad Salstrom, Ron Sararana, William Sawkins, Charley Scandlyn, Ben Selvage, Patrick Sheehan, Steve Shively, Sarah Silva, Todd Slagg, Efrem Smith, Brandon Steiger, Sheri Stirm, Tara Tamblyn, Sheng-Ta Tsai, Stephen Soriano, Brandon Stipe, Chris Thomas, James Underhill, Justin VonSpreckelsen, James Walsh, Derik Watson, Dustin Watson, Katie Wilhite, Matt Williams, Thor Williams, Scott Woods, and Mike Yaconelli.

I am thankful to William Jessup University for allowing me to carve out school time for this book. My gratitude is conveyed to our "best ever" WJU faculty projects coordinator, Emily Darlington, for her willingness in assisting me in the beginning stages of typing the manuscript. Heartfelt thanks to Kelli, Mikal, and Kate, my editors, for their delightful e-mails filled with advice, insights, and fun observations. They made this an enjoyable project.

THANKS

CONTENTS

INTRODUCTION

This book is the result of over 37 years of close association with teenagers and games. Games are great fun, and they build community! Those are the primary reasons we play them and why they've continued to survive in an era when there are so many other forms of entertainment.

This book contains a cross section of both new games and time-honored favorites. Each of the games requires little or no equipment and has been done—either by me or someone I trust—with real kids in a real youth group setting. Whether or not you choose every game for your group, you can rest assured that they have been winners with a group of young people.

Most of these games may be played anywhere, under any condition, and at any time. And you'll rarely need supplies or prep time! Also, the vast majority of these games will work great with all sizes, ages, and types of groups. To help you find the kind of game you're looking for, we've included special icons throughout the book that point out unique qualities. For instance, if you see the "Wide Open" icon next to a game, but you have a medium-sized room, don't avoid that game—just consider how you might adjust it to meet your needs. Take a look at the icons you'll see throughout the book:

 ZOOMER: These games are played at top speed; they're fast and call for lots of energy.

 ENERGY SAVER: These are calmer, more stationary games. They involve a minimum amount of movement.

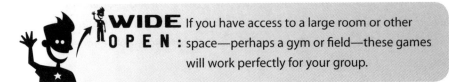

WIDE OPEN : If you have access to a large room or other space—perhaps a gym or field—these games will work perfectly for your group.

PAIR UP: In these games, students form pairs and navigate the game as partners.

CROWD PLEASER: This icon tells you that a game works great with a large group—such as 50 or more students.

Also scattered throughout this book are Gaming Tips, which give essential suggestions and insights on everything from choosing, beginning, to leading a game. Here's one of the most valuable tips right up front: Read the following tip and the other tips carefully, and apply them to your unique group of teenagers.

GAMING TIP: HOW TO ENSURE SAFETY

Treat each young person like your own child, younger sibling, niece, or nephew. Don't put any student in a situation in which you wouldn't readily place this precious family member.

Carry phone numbers of important people who should be contacted in case of an emergency (including ambulance, police, supervisor, parent, and hospital).

Being safe does *not* equal not having much fun. A few minor changes or adjustments can turn a risky game into a safe one without reducing the level of fun.

Obviously games that involve motorized vehicles, slippery surfaces, protruding objects, heavy physical contact, turbulent water, and hitting people in any way deserve special attention before you decide to proceed with your games. Any game is wrong if you know someone will get hurt.

The safety-smart youth leader anticipates danger. Bring your great game idea to life with a simulated run, using youth leaders as "crash test dummies." As you play, you'll be able to identify the danger points and make changes before you present the game to the youth group.

There are a few games I don't play anymore because we know people may be injured. For instance, the game Chubby Bunny involves students filling their mouths with marshmallows (or grapes) one at a time, while repeating the phrase "chubby bunny." Also, the game called 40-Inch Dash involves tying a piece of string to a marshmallow, putting the loose end of the string into one's mouth, and trying to eat one's way to the marshmallow without using hands. Both games have had students gasping for breath. A piece of food could be drawn into the windpipe, causing a student to choke. Beware also of games that involve shooting food into a person's mouth or dropping food into the mouth of a person lying on the floor. (For more unsafe or inappropriate games, see page 140.)

Here are some safety guidelines for your games:
- Avoid using games that encourage any throwing of objects toward another person's face.
- Avoid mixing big and small, weak and strong students in contact sports. The smaller students can get hurt.
- Avoid making everyone in your group play the rougher game. The reluctant participant is often the first one injured.
- Step in and stop a situation that is getting too rowdy, rough, or uncontrolled.

For many games, all that is needed to make them safe is taking time to stop, think, and use common sense. Place spotters around the room so students will not fall. A helpful book on safety you may want to purchase is *Play It Safe: Keeping Your Kids and Your Youth Ministry Alive* by Jack Crabtree.

WHY PLAY GAMES IN A YOUTH GROUP?

Let me suggest seven reasons I think games should be a valuable part of your youth group ministry…

1. Games are universal.

I've traveled a bit, and I can tell you this: Games are a universal language. I've yet to see a country where kids don't want to play games of some sort.

2. Games are ideal come-and-see, entry-level activities.

Games pull new students into your youth group and provide opportunities for a deeper message. Games help tear down emotional walls and get kids mingling and interacting.

3. Games stretch your students, encouraging them to take risks.

Games can help teenagers develop tolerance, persistence, and patience. Games provide a structure within which those virtues can be practiced.

4. Games improve problem-solving skills and help kids deal with life's stresses.

The life of a typical teenager is plenty crowded and complicated. A game provides an oasis of laughter and fun. And depending on the game, there's a chance to do strategic thinking and problem solving.

5. Games build community, acceptance, and a sense of belonging.

Games provide shared experiences that become shared memories. They're inclusive. And if led well, they foster acceptance.

6. Games are relevant.

Games are all over television and the Internet these days, and teenagers account for much of the popularity of media and video games. Games are relevant to your students because games of all kinds are such a familiar part of teenagers' landscape.

7. Games provide good, clean, trouble-free fun.

Teens are hungry for wholesome activities in a positive environment. Life is tough enough; kids need to have fun, play, and laugh together. Games can provide all that and more.

A BRIEF HISTORY OF GAMES

(Stuff you'll want to know if someone asks you why games are a part of your ministry!)

Many games originated as religious rituals, and some date back to the dawn of history. Tug of War, for example, is a dramatized struggle between natural forces, and hopscotch was related to ancient labyrinths and mazes, later adapted to represent the Christian soul's journey from earth to heaven.

We also know that "children in Jesus' day played games similar to hopscotch and jacks. Whistles, rattles, toy animals on wheels, hoops, and spinning tops have been found by archaeologists. Older children and adults found time to play, too, mainly board games. A form of checkers was popular then" (christianitytoday.com).

Much later, in the year 1283, Alfonso X, the king of Castile (and perhaps member of a local Spanish rap group), commissioned a book of games. "Because God wanted man to have every manner of happiness…Wherefore they found and made many types of play and equipment with which to delight themselves," the king declared in the book's introduction.

Then, during the period of Greece's classical glory, no less a luminary than Athenian philosopher Plato praised games as a useful means of teaching children and youth the laws of society. Furthermore, Plato considered games a means of raising young people to become public-spirited and responsible citizens.

Even Columbus, upon his return to Spain in 1496, eagerly told King Ferdinand and Queen Isabella that he'd seen native peoples playing a game with a ball apparently made of gum of a tree which, even though the ball was heavy, would move easily and quickly as if flying. The guy encounters a new world, and what does he want to tell the folks back home? About a rubber ball, that's what. The native people of this new world had demonstrated a trait that is shared by many peoples: using everyday items to create games. People have carved bats from tree limbs, crafted dolls from worn-out socks, whittled toys from scraps of wood, and invented telephones using two tin cans and a piece of string.

Then came the Reformation…

The Reformation accomplished many good things, but I believe it also helped to abolish fun. Games, laughter, and fun—the safety valves of that society—were seen as nonproductive, and nonproductive things had to go. This desire to eliminate the nonproductive helped establish a super-industrious, workaholic world that was inhabited by the very people who believed that people are justified by faith not works. Puritans would tell their children, "Stay busy—you haven't come into the world for pleasure." Yet those children were taught to memorize the Westminster Catechism of 1647, which asks, "What is the chief end of man?" and provides this answer: "To glorify God and enjoy him forever." Apparently enjoying God and having fun weren't exactly compatible. In some circles today, it's still thought that "fun" and "church" shouldn't be in the same sentence.

A Few Philosophical Thoughts on Games

As children, we stayed in good physical shape because we were always playing in the yard, riding bikes, jumping rope, swimming, or climbing trees. And we stayed in good mental shape because our play provided a workout for our imaginations.

We became the characters in our forts, the dolls in our dollhouses, the soldiers on our battlefields, the sports heroes in our stadiums. We lived all that we imagined as we vicariously placed ourselves in the situations we'd imagined.

Then we grew up and shelved our imaginations so we could engage the "real" world.

Let me confess: This book is more than a compilation of fun games to play with a group. In many ways, it's a cry for all of us to develop richer imaginations, tapping into our God-given creativity. I believe play is necessary for good mental and physical health. Play relieves stress, boosts self-esteem, and builds community.

I'll bet you need all three of those play-benefits in your life. I know I do.

Yet games and play are disappearing from our ministries—for several reasons.

First of all, many games that were formerly played for fun have evolved into professional sports. In spite of what a nation of couch potatoes tells you, watching someone play a sport is not the same thing as playing a game yourself.

What distinguishes a true game from a professional sport is in part whether the primary goal of the participant is to have fun or to make a living. For example, consider the game of lawn tennis. In 1905, ladies played lawn tennis in full skirts and long sleeves, with natty little straw hats perched on their heads. The game was a fun social event. A hundred years later, leading women players are highly trained athletes, engaged in severe competition.

Much of the lighthearted joy of games has disappeared; competitive sport has taken its place and only the extremely talented are invited to play while the rest of us watch. Don't let this happen in your youth group! Games need to be played, not observed! Don't let the gifted athletes siphon the joy out of the game for the "average" players.

When is the last time you saw a professional athlete laugh frequently and joyfully during a game? Amateurs do it all the time! It happens so often when friends get together for a round of golf, or a game of badminton, that it's not unusual for a game to be suspended until the laughter subsides and participants can resume play.

At the professional and near-professional level, games are played with such intensity they sometimes cease to be games at all. To be truly and fully fun, games must be played for fun—by amateurs. The laughter of teenagers at play is communal, gregarious, and contagious—and you don't need to be a pro to play.

Secondly, play is disappearing because the activities described by many teenagers as "fun" are solitary experiences. You don't need to organize a team to fire up a high-tech, battery-powered gadget. The typical teenager's bedroom contains a computer, TV, DVD player, and video game system; there's no need to interact with another person to play.

The result: Your students are losing their ability to play. Plus they're forfeiting the character-developing opportunities that come with face-to-face social interactions. Now, more than ever, we must seek ways to incorporate into our ministries games that will foster a common bond between students.

A third reason play is disappearing from our ministries is that we're getting older. And when I say "older," I don't necessarily mean chronological age. Some 23-year-old youth leaders have become frustrated with the energetic, unpredictable kids who attracted them to youth ministry in the first place. It's all about attitude.

I've noticed that many youth workers have forgotten how much fun it is to work with playful, energetic young people. These are the same youth leaders who insist they want students to move beyond "fun and games." I'm in agreement; it would be unwise to have a youth group based solely on fun and games. However, to eliminate fun and games altogether would be equally unwise. To get rid of youthful fun because it's no longer enjoyable for a few older youth leaders is criminal.

Fourthly, play is disappearing in youth ministry because we're fearful of labels. Specifically, many youth leaders are fearful of being identified as "a kid who never grew up." I've always believed the best youth leaders are two-thirds adult and one-third kid. Don't reverse this equation or you'll quickly be in deep weeds! But don't forget to honor that third of you that's still looking to call up some friends and go out to play. It's your ticket to building relationships with teenagers and having a blast while you do it.

A Theology of Fun and Games

Of the 156 episodes from *The Twilight Zone* series, one of my favorites is "Kick the Can." Originally shown on February 9, 1962, the story is about a group of older people living in a retirement home. Charles and Ben have been friends since childhood, and when some children playing Kick the Can outside their retirement home capture their attention, Charles shares a secret.

The secret of youth, Charles tells the other residents, is in playing games. Charles finally gets the rest of the retirees to play when he says in desperation, "I can't play Kick the Can alone."

But his best friend Ben won't play. Ben thinks playing isn't something older people should do.

Charles' reply is priceless. He tells Ben that Ben's afraid to look silly, afraid to make a mistake. Charles says, "You decided you were an old man, and that has made you old." Reluctantly, Charles goes off to play Kick the Can without Ben.

The episode ends with the retirement home residents transformed into children again, happily playing together, while Ben has remained an old man.

When we allow ourselves to play as children do, we can feel God's pleasure fill our lungs. We instinctively recognize that playing games is one way to do as Paul urged us—to "rejoice in the Lord always" (Philippians 4:4).

Yet, how often do we allow our teenagers to do just that?

Too many religious people are so serious that they act as if they haven't smiled in years. To them, playful interaction is an inconvenience and anything not driven by purpose isn't worth the time. We're supposed to be a community of joy and grace, but somehow we've lost the elements of spontaneity and mystery. We have become a community of programs.

We need to have fun and play games because God commands us to rest from work; to break the pattern of work and its grip on our daily lives, schedules, and thinking. Those of us who value play have a biblical basis for seeing play as important: "There is a time for everything, and a season for every activity under heaven…a time to weep and a time to laugh, a time to mourn and a time to dance" (Ecclesiastes 3:1-4).

I don't think the average person can imagine Jesus as someone who laughed and knew the true meaning of fun. Most art and media usually portray Jesus as stern and unsmiling. Yet isn't he the Creator of our ability to smile and laugh in the first place? And since Jesus was fully human as well as divine, we can safely assume Jesus loved a good, hearty laugh now and again.

Read the Gospels and you'll see Christ's sly insertions of humor and sharp wit and appreciation of the absurd. Jesus employed irony in his sermons (see Matthew 7:16). He often used deliberately preposterous statements to get his point across (see Matthew 18:23-25 and Mark 10:25).

I've always enjoyed a certain story attributed to Erma Bombeck (although I've never been able to track her down as the source for the story). It seems Ms. Bombeck was approached by a woman from church who said, "We know that Jesus never laughed because the Bible never says he laughed." Ms. Bombeck's quick reply was "Neither does it say in the Bible that Jesus wet his pants, but if he was ever two years old we can assume that happened."

I agree with Ms. Bombeck: You can't make an argument that Jesus was always solemn by looking at Scripture. You can, however, see trace elements of his humor as you see how he responded to and talked with people.

Plus, Jesus had a soft spot in his heart for children, and that says plenty. In Matthew 18:2-5 we read about an incident where Jesus called a child to him. Jesus put the child in the midst of very serious adults and said, "I tell you the truth, unless you change and become like little children, you will never enter the kingdom of heaven. Therefore, whoever humbles himself like this child is the greatest in the kingdom of heaven. And whoever welcomes a little child like this in my name welcomes me."

Humility is the singular, small door to the divine playground of fun. To enter the kingdom, we must bow down our high and holy heads. That's the only way. If you're standing proud, you can't clear the doorway. The kingdom has been prepared for those who come to it as little children (Mark 10:15).

What if children really are examples of true faith? What if working with young people also involves learning from them?

In addition to Erma Bombeck, deep theological thinkers have enjoyed play…or wished they did.

Martin Luther wrote, "It is pleasing to the dear Lord whenever thou rejoicest or laughest from the bottom of thy heart" (*Surprised by Laughter: the Comic World of C.S. Lewis,* Terry Lindvall). Sounds like a guy I'd want at the next youth retreat during game time.

I believe only the innocent (children) or those liberated from guilt are really free and able to play. We've long been like bathers who want to keep their feet, or at least one foot, or by all means one toe, on the bottom so they stay grounded. To lose that foothold would be to surrender ourselves to a glorious tumble into the surf.

And you know what? That's not a bad thing.

When a person makes a faith commitment to Jesus, repentance from sin often results in initial sadness that swiftly becomes a spontaneous gladness mixed with laughter. Why? Because our sins have been forgiven!

The proper response to receiving new life is joy. Humility accepts grace with wild abandon; laughter and joy follow repentance as sunrise follows night. Like David before the Ark of God, we should kick up our heels in delight (see 2 Samuel 6:14). As the psalmist tells us, "Our mouths were filled with laughter, our tongues with songs of joy" (Psalm 126:2a).

Hang on to the giggles, laughter, and teaching moments that happen in your youth room. These are important memories your students will need when they face tough situations.

People who've learned to play—and play well with others—are ahead of the pack. "I would much rather be ruled by men who know how to play than by men who do not know how to play," G.K. Chesterton writes in *All Things Considered*. "[The playground] is a place for humanising those who might otherwise be tyrants, or even experts."

And one of the tragedies of C.S. Lewis' life was that he had discouraging experiences with games as a child in school. Those experiences negatively colored his view of games for the rest of his life. In his book *Surprised by Joy,* Lewis wrote: "Compulsory games had, in my day, banished the element of play…The rivalry was too fierce, the prizes too glittering, the 'hell of failure' too severe." C.S. Lewis possessed a heightened sense of play and fun throughout his life, but because he felt inadequate, he didn't participate in games while young.

If we hope to build relationships with teenagers, perhaps we adults would do well to relearn the lost language of youth—the language of play.

Play is one way to celebrate, to let the laughter spill out of your life. It's also a healthy way to let off steam or take a break from pain that surrounds us. It also helps us grow closer to each other and ultimately to God. Guide your students through the games in this book with these ideas in your heart and mind.

PLAY WELL WITH OTHERS

GAMES

19

"A" WAS AN APPLE PIE

Supplies: none

Have your students sit in a circle and in turn add a verb beginning with the next letter of the alphabet. For instance, the leader says, "A was an apple pie. A ate it."

In rotation the other players add things like "B bought it," "C cooked it," "D dunked it," and so on, through something like "Z zoomed it."

ACTING ADVERBS

Supplies: none

This game involves some simple acting.

Choose one player to be "It." Ask the player to leave the room, and when "It" is safely out of range, have the other players choose an adverb such as *humorously, gracefully,* or *furiously.* They're not to reveal the adverb to "It."

Call "It" back into the room and ask "It" to discover the word by asking players to do different things in the manner of the adverb. For example, "It" may ask various players to eat, walk, dance, read, or jump—each in accordance with the chosen adverb.

If "It" can't guess the word after asking everybody to do something, reveal the adverb and choose another "It" for the next round.

Here's a twist to simplify and speed up this game: Allow "It" to guess a synonym rather than the exact adverb. For example, if the adverb is "furiously," and "It" guesses "angrily," count the response as a correct answer.

How to Select a Game (Part One)

First off, know your group's culture and know your group's interests. Just because you heard something was a big hit at a youth ministry on the other side of the country, don't assume it'll be the same in yours.

Questions to help determine which game will best suit your group include:

- How many people are expected?
- What equipment or supplies are required?
- What are the ages of the students?
- What is the physical ability of the students?
- Where will the game take place?
- What is the time of day?
- How much space do we have?
- How much time do we have?
- What will the weather be like?

GAMING TIP

AFFINITIES

Supplies: paper, pens or pencils

Within a stated time, each player must write down as many familiar affinities (words commonly joined by "and") as possible. Examples include "Adam and Eve" and "Alpha and Omega."

Game Twist: Each player is provided with a list of unfinished affinities, such as Adam and _____, Alpha and _____.

ALL ACROSS

Supplies: none

"It" stands between two goal lines or tape marks about 30 feet apart and calls "All across!" All the players cross from one line to the other and "It" tags them as they run across. Now the players are on the other side of the field and must run back to their original side, passing "It" and those who have been tagged by "It." The game continues until everybody has been tagged and is in the middle of the field or area. All who are caught assist until everyone is in the middle together.

Game Twist: Have only guys or only girls stand in a row on a line. The "capture" (instead of tagging) is made by lifting the person off the ground until "1-2-3" is counted. Or play "Gorilla and the Trees," where "It" is the gorilla and can move all around the field. Those tagged become trees and can only move one step in any direction, using their arms like branches to tag those who run back and forth.

ALL RUN

Supplies: ball (any kind)

"It" stands with the ball, and the other players gather close. "It" tosses the ball high into the air and the other players flee in any direction. "It" catches the ball and tosses it at the runners. A runner hit by the ball trades places with "It." If the ball does not make contact with anyone, "It" tosses the ball up again.

Game Twist: "It" catches the ball and calls "Halt." The runners must then stand still. The players must not move their feet at any time, but they can move their bodies. Or form a circle and have students number off. One person stands in the center of the circle, throws the ball into the air, and calls out a number. Whoever has that number runs for the ball as everyone else tries to run as far away as they can. The person running for the ball reaches it, yells out "halt," and everyone else stops running. The person who has the ball then takes three steps toward anyone and tosses the ball at him or her.

ALPHABET GAME

Supplies: none

Have students form pairs, and assign a topic for conversation. (Some examples: describe yesterday; describe your favorite restaurants; describe your favorite movies.) One partner will begin the conversation with one sentence about the assigned topic. The second person will comment on what the first person said or add another comment on the topic. These one-sentence conversations go back and forth between the partners. The catch is that each participant has to begin a sentence using successive letters of the alphabet. Pairs don't have to start with the letter A. In fact, it's more challenging if you have pairs start with another letter and work their way back around to the starting letter. Pairs try to go as fast as they can to get through all the letters of the alphabet.

How to Select a Game (Part Two)

Look for games that are fun to describe, fun to watch, and fun to play. If you select a game that may naturally become competitive, make sure it requires little or no skill. Choose games where everyone is on an equal footing. These are games where there's no "first string." For example, choose a game in which everyone plays each position for a period of time, everyone gets to shoot, or everyone must touch the ball before a shot is taken.

GAMING TIP

ALPHABET POCKETS

Supplies: items found among the players

Have students form groups of four to six. Everyone in the group should search through his or her own pocket, wallet, bag, and purse. The group tries to come up with one possession that begins with each letter of the alphabet.

ALPHABET SOUP

Supplies: none

Have students form groups of eight to10, and have each group choose a guiding coach. You will yell out a letter of the alphabet to all the teams. When the groups hear the letter, they should try as quickly as possible to form that letter lying on the floor using their bodies (coaches excluded). Coaches help in directing the other team members to their proper places and announce when the team has finished.

ANATOMY CLUMPS

Supplies: none

Yell out a body part and a number. Students connect that part of the body (hands, feet, or elbows) in a group with that number of people (fives, threes, eights). Everyone runs to form groups as quickly as possible.

ANATOMY SHUFFLE

Supplies: none

Have your students form pairs and make two concentric circles—one circle inside the other. At your mark, the outside circle moves clockwise and the inside circle moves counterclockwise. After a few moments, shout something like "finger, foot!" The partner from the inside circle finds his or her partner from the outside circle, who must stop altogether and remain in one position. The first body part called is always the inner circle's instruction, and the second body part is the outer circle's instruction. So, once the inside partner finds a partner, the pair touches a finger (inner circle partner) to a foot (outer circle partner).

Other examples might include combinations such as: "hand, ear" or "elbow, nose" or "nose, armpit."

(Game adapted from Wayne Rice and Mike Yaconelli, *Play It!*)

Game Twist: Try Knight Rider, Donkey, Princess.

When the music stops, yell out either "Knight Rider," "Donkey," or "Princess." The objective is for partners to find each other as quick as possible and get into the specific position of Knight Rider, Donkey, or Princess. Descriptions of positions:

- Knight Rider: One person piggybacks a partner.
- Princess: One person gets on bended knee and the partner sits on the knee.
- Donkey: One person gets on all fours while the partner hops on the back.

ANIMAL, VEGETABLE, OR MINERAL

Supplies: none

Begin the game by thinking of a subject and telling the other players that you are thinking of either animal (including humans and animal products, such as fur and eggs), vegetable (including all types of plants and their products, such as cereal and wood), or mineral (including glass, stone, and metal). The other players take turns asking questions that can be answered "yes," "no," or "sometimes," until one of them guesses the subject correctly. That person starts the next game. There is no limit on the number of questions, but I suggest an allotted five-minute time period.

Game Twist: One player leaves the room while the others agree on a subject. The player returns, and the others inform him that the subject is either animal, vegetable, or mineral. The player then asks questions until he discovers the answer.

ANKLE BALLOON POP

Supplies: easily breakable balloon, piece of string or yarn

Give everyone a small, easily breakable balloon and a piece of string or yarn. Have them each blow up the balloon and tie it to their ankle. The string should be about 10 inches long (between the ankle and the balloon). Then announce that they are to try to stomp out other people's balloons while keeping their own safe.

APPLIANCES

Supplies: none

Have students form groups of five to 10 students. Privately assign each group an imaginary room in a typical home, such as the garage, living room, kitchen, bathroom, laundry room, or outside shed. The group is to then select an appliance, machine, or tool in that room and create a working, moving model of the machine. The catch is, they can use only their bodies and any props available in your meeting room. After a few minutes of planning, each team gets up and acts out its machine, and the other groups try to guess what it is.

AROUND THE WORLD PING-PONG

Supplies: Ping-Pong table (or similar), Ping-Pong paddles, and ball

Here's a good way to add some excitement to an ordinary game of Ping-Pong. Have up to a dozen students stand around a regular Ping-Pong table. One player should be on each end of the table; the other players are at the sides. The first person serves the ball, just like regular Ping-Pong, but after the serve, that player puts the paddle down on the table (with the handle sticking over the edge). The next person in line (to the server's right) picks up the paddle and waits for the ball to be returned. The line keeps rotating around the table in a clockwise fashion, with each person hitting the ball once from whichever end of the table he or she happens to be. When someone drops the paddle, misses the ball, or hits it off the table, that player steps out of this round. When the last two people are playing, they must hit the ball, put the paddle down, turn completely around, pick up the paddle, and hit the ball again.

BACK ARTIST

Supplies: paper, marker

This game is based on the old "telephone game" but involves touch rather than hearing. No talking is allowed. Divide the group into teams of four to six. Each team sits in a line, behind each other. The last person in each team is shown a simple drawing of an object (such as a house, star, duck, cat, dog, or Christmas tree). Children's coloring books can provide more ideas. The person who sees the drawing then tries to draw an exact copy of it, using fingers, on the back of the person in front of the drawer. The drawing can only be done once. The second person then draws on the back of the person in front of him or her. This continues until the person at the front of the line draws what he or she felt on a piece of paper with a marker. The final picture rarely looks like the original!

Game Twist: Have the students form pairs and sit back to back. Give one person in each pair a simple drawing (without letting the other partner see it), and give the other partner a blank piece of paper and a pen. The person with the simple drawing must verbally communicate to the other person what is on the paper, and the partner must make an exact copy of it on his or her own paper.

BACK TO BACK

Supplies: none

Have your students form pairs and have them sit on the floor back to back. (This works best when the partners are of similar size.) Have everyone pull their knees up to their chest with their feet flat on the floor and their arms linked with their partners'. Then tell pairs to stand up. With a little timing and cooperation, it shouldn't be too hard.

Then combine pairs into foursomes. Have the foursomes sit on the floor back-to-back-to-back-to-back with arms linked. Tell foursomes to stand up. It is a little harder with four. Keep adding more people to the group until the giant blob of students can't stand up anymore.

Game Twist: Try "Face to Face," where partners sit facing each other and holding hands, with their knees up to their chests and toes to each other's toes. They should try to stand up.

BALLOON BASKETBALL

Supplies: large balloon, chairs

Arrange your chairs in rows with every other row facing the opposite direction. There should be the same number of people on each of the two teams that are playing. One team faces in one direction; the second team the other direction. The two rows of chairs on each end should face inward. There can be any number of players on a team.

After all the players are seated in their team's chairs, toss a large 11-inch or 16-inch balloon (see Gaming Tip) into the center of the players. The players cannot stand, but they must try to bat the balloon with their hands into the end zone that they are facing. As soon as the balloon drops into the end zone over the heads of the last row of people, the team going that direction gets points. If the balloon goes out of bounds, throw it back into the center.

(Game adapted from Wayne Rice and Mike Yaconelli, *Play It!*)

How to Include Balloons in Your Games

Balloons provide an inexpensive good time; use them as often as you can. Here are some balloon tips:

• Buy balloons in stores that specialize in balloons. Look up "balloons" in the yellow pages or on the Internet—you may be surprised at the number of balloon stores.

• Stretch balloons before blowing them up. This makes them easier to inflate.

• The higher the quality of the balloon, the harder it is to inflate (better balloons are made of thicker latex). The good news is that these balloons last longer.

• When it's cold, balloons are harder to inflate. But when it's hot outside, the opposite is true. When it's hot, you can easily over-expand a balloon and pop it.

• You can tell when a balloon is inflated to full capacity because it gets rather transparent, and you can feel the tightness of the latex.

• If you're playing rough games with balloons, they'll be able to take more abuse if they're underinflated.

• Most people know the basics about tying off a balloon once it's inflated. But there's a trick to it: After inflating the balloon, hold the neck in one hand, pinching it shut between thumb and first finger. With your free hand, stretch the neck up and twist it a few times. Then tie it off. The twisting keeps the air from escaping after it's tied.

BALLOON BOP

Supplies: balloon, small object such as marble or candy

Have students form teams of four to eight, and have each team stand in a circle holding hands. For each team, place a marble or small piece of candy in a balloon. Inflate and tie the balloon. Toss the marble-filled balloon into each team's circle. Students will attempt to keep the balloon in the air without letting go of each other's hands. The marble-filled balloon will move in unexpected ways.

BALLOON HEAD

Supplies: 2 large boxes, balloons

Place two large empty boxes at opposite ends of a room. Have a large quantity of inflated balloons on the floor, in the center of the room. Divide your group into two teams, and position teams at opposite ends of the room. When the game begins, each team tries to put the balloons into its box—which is located at the *other* end of the room. Here's the catch: Students can only use heads (no arms, hands, legs, feet, or mouths)!

BALLOON LAUNCHERS

Supplies: balloons, water, 5 feet of surgical tubing that's a half-inch diameter (you can get this from a medical supply company), funnel with a 6-inch diameter mouth, four 1-inch hose clamps, drill, duct tape

To make inexpensive water balloon launchers, drill two holes on opposite sides of the funnel. The holes should be three-eighths-inch in diameter and about one-quarter-inch below the rim of the funnel. Cut the tubing in half and feed 3 inches of the first length into one hole. Then slip the hose clamp onto both ends of the tube to join them together. Tighten the hose clamp. Then repeat this process with the other length of tubing. At the other end, fold over the tubing to make a handle and use the other hose clamp to solidify it.

Now use some duct tape to make a cradle inside the funnel. Without this part, when the balloon is released, it will squeeze down inside the hole and burst.

Water balloon launchers can also be purchased on the Internet. Type in "water balloon launcher" in your search engine and discover several sites that sell launcher kits.

Fill the balloons with water, and let your students have fun by aiming and launching the balloons! Be sure to carefully oversee this activity. Note: Be kind to the environment and have your kids pick up any balloon fragments after the game.

BALLOON NOSE BLOW

Supplies: balloons

Give students balloons and challenge them to each blow up and pop a balloon using their noses.

(Game adapted from Jonathan McKee's Web site, *www.thesource4ym.com*)

BANANA PEELING

Supplies: blindfolds, bananas

Two blindfolded players (ask for volunteers) stand toe-to-toe, each peel a banana, and feed it to the other. Remind students to dress for the mess!

BARNYARD

Supplies: paper, pen or pencil

In an empty area with no chairs or other obstacles, give each player a folded piece of paper with the name of an animal written on it (such as pig, horse, cow, chicken, duck, dog, sheep, frog, cat, cricket, or any other animal that makes a distinct noise). To ensure equal teams, assign the same six animals to every six people.

Students are not to say a word. When the lights are turned out, everyone is to immediately make the sound of his or her animal. As soon as students find someone else who is making the same noise, they lock arms and try to find others making the same sound. When the lights come back on, everyone sits down in their groups.

(Game adapted from Wayne Rice and Mike Yaconelli, *Play It!*)

BARNYARD CHORUS

Supplies: none

This is not exactly a game of skill, but it does provide a wonderful excuse to make a lot of noise! One player starts by saying that he or she has some cows. This student starts to moo. Another player says he or she has some roosters and immediately begins to crow. The other players then tell what animal they own and start to make the right (or nearly right) sounds for those animals. In the end everybody is going at full volume, trying to drown out the others.

How to Lead Messy Games

Have you ever noticed that you often can measure the level of fun little children have had by the amount of dirt, grass stains, or paint on their bodies? Sometimes teenagers, too, need to dive in and get dirty to have fun.

We often shy away from the messy type of games in fear of the potential repercussions from various church committees. But if we plan properly, openly communicate our purposes, and schedule cleanup times, we can have a blast.

If you will be playing messy games, let the students know in advance by advertising that they will need to "dress for the mess." If you don't, then only a few students will participate. Those inexpensive-looking jeans cost $110, that ripped T-shirt costs $39, and those old-looking shoes cost $195. Teenagers don't want to have their favorite and expensive clothes wrecked. But, if they know in advance, they'll dress accordingly. Also, if you are playing messy games, have towels and changing rooms nearby for emergencies. It might be helpful to have a playing area covered with a tarp or dropcloth to protect floors. You may also want to have a cleanup crew handy to wipe up spills immediately so no one slips and hurts themselves.

BEANS AND TOOTHPICKS

Supplies: plates, beans, toothpicks, table, chairs

All the players sit around a table or several tables. In front of each player, set a plate containing 10 beans and two toothpicks. Students will use the toothpicks to lift the beans from the plate and put them on the table. The game may continue until students get all 10 beans to the table.

BEAT THE CLOCK

BEAT THE CLOCK

Supplies: stopwatch or timer

Have your students sit in a circle and hold hands. One designated player in the circle will say "start," and you'll hit a stopwatch or timer. The players in the circle, beginning with the person who says "start," each squeeze the hand of the person to the right, until the squeeze goes all the way around the circle to the person who started. This person will say "stop," and you'll stop the time. The group will try to go around the circle as fast as they can. Have them try it again to beat their last record!

BEDLAM

BEDLAM

Supplies: none

This game requires groups of equal size. Each group stands in one corner of the room or playing field. The play area can be either square or rectangular. At a signal from you, each group attempts to move as quickly as possible to the corner diagonal from it. Each group must also perform a specific action as they go. The activities can include: walking backward, wheelbarrow racing (one person is the wheelbarrow), piggyback, rolling somersaults, hopping on one foot, skipping, or crab-walking.

There will be mass bedlam in the center as all four teams crisscross. (Do not have students simply run across because that's a little boring, and they are more likely to get hurt.)

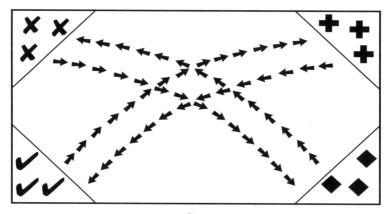

BELLYBUTTON BASKETBALL

Supplies: small handheld fish net, rubber band, rubber ball

Bend the handle of a fish net (one used in a home aquarium) so that it fits securely in the front of your pants with the net straight out in front. Attach a rubber ball with a rubber band attached to it at the base of the net. (Remember those old ball and paddle games? Just remove the string and ball and use with the fish net.)

Teenagers must swing the ball into the net without using their hands.

(Game adapted from Jonathan McKee's Web site, *www.thesource4ym.com*)

BIG MOUTH

Supplies: none

All you need is an open area. Get the students to line up, and explain that the object of the game is to run as far as they can and at the same time scream at the top of their lungs. When they run out of air, they have to stop running. Have the whole group run at once. The player who runs the farthest (screams the longest with one breath) is the "big mouth."

BIRD, BEAST, FISH

Supplies: none

Players sit in a circle with a caller (you) standing in the center. Point to any student and say, "Bird, beast, fish—fish!" or "Bird, beast, fish—bird!" Or "Bird, beast, fish—beast!"

Then count to 10 and the player pointed to must name a kind of fish (or bird or beast—whatever is the last type of animal you said). If the student can't name an animal, then he or she takes your place in the center of the circle. If the student does name an animal, you remain in the center and call on a different person to name another animal. Animals cannot be repeated during the game.

Game Twist: Try "Earth, Air, Fire, and Water," where the student in the center picks someone in the circle and calls out one of the following: "Earth," "Air," "Fire," or "Water." By the count of 10, the person called upon must name a creature, not already named, that walks on the ground, flies in the air, or swims in the water. If "Fire" is called, everyone changes seats.

How to Do a Pre-Game Checklist
Some things to make sure of before leading a game:
- If you've never played or seen the specific game, test it before you use it.
  Go over the directions for the game carefully beforehand, and practice giving them with some close friends to be sure you will be completely understood.
- Have the room and all supplies ready, and mark off any necessary boundaries. Also, have any starting and finish lines drawn.
- Select people to assist in the game; choose youth leaders or other volunteers who are enthusiastic and love to have fun. In order to have teenagers excited about a game, the leaders need to be jazzed about it, too!
- Set up early so that you can be free to greet the students as they arrive. This also shows them that you are prepared and ready to have fun.
- Delegate necessary tasks to volunteers (or students) so that each person is responsible for something.

BIRDS FLY

Supplies: none

Say "Birds fly," wave your arms in a flying motion three or four times, then drop your arms to your sides. All of the students follow your example.

Name a bird, beast, or fish while waving your arms. For example, "Cats fly," "Ducks fly," "Worms fly," "Elephants fly," "Moths fly," or "Crabs fly." The students, however, should wave their arms only when anything that *can* fly is named. You try to confuse your students by moving your arms at the wrong time.

Game Twist: Say "Cats meow" with appropriate sounds or gestures that students must imitate. Continue, "Hens cluck," "Sheep baa," and so on, each time with an appropriate gesture or sound. At some point, substitute a false statement and motion such as "Cows bark" or "Elephants fly." The players should try their best not to imitate the false motions or sounds at any time.

How to Choose Cooperative Games

Cooperative games bring people together so that when the game is over, the players are better friends than when they started. Look for games in which cooperation among players is necessary. In cooperative games, you play *with* one another rather than *against* one another. The emphasis should be on having fun. During this kind of cooperative game, winning becomes almost irrelevant or anticlimactic.

You can often turn competitive games into cooperative ones with a bit of adaptation. For example, change the classic game King of the Mountain into People of the Mountain. Rather than all the players trying to be the only one on top of the mountain, try to get everyone on top of the mountain.

We've done this with a 3x3-foot sturdy wooden table top that is one foot off the ground. We have had up to 12 kids on it at one time. Let me know if you beat that record!

GAMING TIP

BLIND ANIMAL

Supplies: paper, marker, tape, index cards, pencils

As students arrive, write their names on paper in large letters and tape the names to their backs. Tell them not to let anyone else see the papers. When all the students have arrived, give them index cards and pencils. They are to write down as many other students' names as possible, while trying not to let anyone get theirs. There is only one rule: No one is allowed to stand with his or her back against anything.

In situations where all the students know each other, instead put names of animals on their backs. For instance, if a student is a rhinoceros, anyone who found it out would write on his own card the name of the student *and* the word *rhinoceros.*

BODY BALLOON BURST

Supplies: pens or pencils, slips of paper, balloons

Write each of the following body parts on separate slips of paper (enough for everybody to have one slip): right hand, left hand, mouth, right foot, left foot, and rear end. Give each student one slip of paper.

Have students identify themselves by doing one of the following actions: hands (raise appropriate hand and shake it), feet (hop on appropriate foot), rear end (shake it), or mouth (yell "I'm a mouth"). On your signal, have them form groups and form a body (two feet, two hands, one rear end, and one mouth).

The feet then carry one of the hands to you. You give the hand a balloon. The feet carry the hand back to the mouth. Two hands hold the balloon. Mouth blows it up. Hands tie it off. Rear end sits on it and pops it!

BOWLING PIN KNOCK OVER

Supplies: 2-liter soda bottles or bowling pins (1 for every 5 students), soft balls

Have students form into two groups and gather on opposite ends of the room. Place the bottles on the floor a few feet from the back wall of each group. Using relatively soft balls, the object of the game is to knock over the opposing group's bottles. Anyone who can get a ball may throw it at the bottles or pass the ball to a group mate. The only restriction is that all group members must remain in their half of the court. Defenders may block a ball by catching it or by stopping it with any part of their body. When a bottle is down it stays down, although students may slide it to one side to get it out of the way. Students are allowed to stand around the pins but must not come closer than 5 feet at any time.

Game Twist: Play with several different types of balls; try volleyballs, soccer balls, tennis balls, and so on.

BROOM TWIST RELAY

Supplies: broom

Students are lined up in teams of five to eight people. Some 20 or 30 feet away, a team leader holds a broom. When the game begins, each player runs to the team leader, takes the broom, and holds it against the chest with the bristles up in the air over the player's head. Looking up at the broom, the player must turn around as fast as possible seven times, while the leader counts the number of turns. Then the player hands the broom back to the leader, runs back to the team, and tags the next player. Players become very dizzy!

For the utmost safety, ask youth leaders or volunteers to run alongside the students and act as spotters ready to catch them or break their fall.

Game Twist: Have students run to a bat, keep the bat on the ground with hand on top of bat and forehead on back of hand, spin around seven times, then run back and tag the next person.

BUILDING SENTENCES

Supplies: none

Have students form groups of seven to 10. Group members should get into a circle. The object is for each group to form a sentence in which every word begins with the same letter. One person in each group begins by saying the first word, and the rest of the words must also begin with the same letter as that first word. Students will say words in order around the circle, until it reaches the person who started. That person will end the sentence. Each player must be careful not to give a word that completes the sentence, as the starting person is the only one who can finish the sentence. For example the first person says "An," the second person says "angry," the third person says "ape," the fourth person says "ate," and so on until a sentence is formed similar to this one: "An angry ape ate attractive, audacious, ancient April apples." This sentence is absurd, but the more ridiculous, the greater the fun.

BULL IN THE RING

Supplies: none

Have students stand in a circle, facing inward and holding hands. Appoint one player to be the "bull," and place this student in the center of the ring. At your signal, the "bull" tries to break out of the ring by charging the players' arms so their clasped hands are forced apart. When the "bull" is successful in getting out, the two players whose hands were forced apart give chase and attempt to catch the "bull" within a designated area. The player catching and tagging the "bull" becomes the "bull" in the next round.

Game Twist: Have all the players chase the "bull" after he or she breaks free.

BUMPETY-BUMP-BUMP

Supplies: none

The players stand or sit in a large circle. Have one player act as "It" for every 10 players in the circle. The "Its" are in the center of the circle.

Give students a moment to learn the names of their neighbors on either side. The "Its" should then run up to anyone in the circle, point to him or her, and say, "Right—bumpety, bump, bump," to which the player pointed to must instantly respond with the name of the person to the player's right. If the player fails to respond before "It" finishes saying, "Bumpety, bump, bump," the player changes places with the "It" who pointed to him or her.

Likewise, if "It" says, "Left—bumpety, bump, bump" the player would respond with the name of the person to the player's left.

How to Determine the Role of "It"

The best way to find the person who will play the role of "It" during a game is for you to ask for volunteers. If the games have been fun, teenagers will be begging, "Choose me! Choose me!"

Or you can try other fun activities to select the person who will be "It." You hold as many blades of grass in hand as there are players in the game. One of the blades of grass is shorter than the others, but they are arranged in your hand so they appear to be uniform length. Each player draws a blade of grass; the one who picks the short blade of grass is "It."

Or players take a broomstick, baseball bat, or walking stick. One by one, in rapid succession—and in no particular order—each player wraps a hand around the broomstick, starting at the bottom just above the broom. (The sides of the fists must touch.) Up and up they go until there is just enough room at the top of the stick for one full fist. The player who secures this position is "It."

Playing the role of "It" for great lengths of time can be embarrassing to some individuals. To eliminate this possibility, the number of times "It" remains in the role should be set before the game begins. "It" is then permitted to select another person to take his place while he joins the group.

GAMING TIP

 # BUZZ

Supplies: none

Have students form groups of four to six students, and have group members sit together in a circle. One of the students in each group should start the game by saying, "one." Moving around the circle, the others in turn will say, "two," "three," "four," "five," and "six." But when "seven" is reached, that player must instead say "buzz." The counting then continues around the circle with "eight," but each time there is a multiple of seven or any number with a seven in it, the player must say "Buzz" instead of the number. (So at 7, 14, 17, 21, 27, 28, 35, 37, 42, and 47 the person must say "Buzz.") The goal is to count to 50 without making a mistake. If students make a mistake they must start over again.

Take it to the next level: Same as Buzz, but with the addition of saying "fizz" instead of five and multiples of five (5, 10, 15, 20, 25, 30, 35, 40, 45, 50). For the number 35 (a multiple of 7 and 5) the player says "buzz-fizz."

CAN-CAN BUMP

Supplies: clean, plastic garbage can (about 3 feet tall)

This game is seriously tiring, but it is one of my favorites. Form a circle of five to 25 students. This is not a co-ed game and is best played with guys or girls only. Have students hold hands around a clean, plastic garbage can. They should begin pulling and tugging, but not letting go. They are trying to get someone else to bump into the can. If a player touches the can in any way, that player is out. If players break their grip on one another, they are both out. Play pauses after each player leaves the circle, giving much needed time for players to rest and re-grip their handholds. Play until one person remains. A safety measure for this game would be to put down wrestling mats or anything else that's available to make a soft, cushiony surface.

Game Twist: Add another trash can to speed up the game.

Instead of having students hold hands, ask them to hold connectors such as rolled up T-shirts or foot-long nylon ropes with knots in each end.

You might also have students form equal teams. Alternate the students in the circle so that no two team members are next to each other.

How to Introduce a Game

- Introduce games in a way that arouses interest and creates anticipation. Lead games with enthusiasm, starting out excited and staying excited. Have fun with your students!
- Never ask students if they'd like to play a particular game. Someone is likely to shout "No!" or suggest another game, resulting in confusion. Instead, confidently move ahead to explain the game you've decided to play.
- Don't tell the group, "We're going to play a game." The best way to ruin a game is by telling kids you're going to play a game! And certainly don't introduce the type of game, such as: "OK, now we're going to play a mixer." How much fun does that sound like it'll be? And does the average middle schooler even know what a mixer is?
- Put students in their playing positions *before* you begin to describe a game. Form students into teams, lines, circles, pairs, or whatever. This allows the group to start playing immediately after your explanation.
- When starting a game, just start doing it. For example, say: "Before we get started today I want everyone on this side of the room to scoot one foot that way while we run this rope between you…" Ten minutes later kids will be looking at each other saying, "Hey, we're playing games! Cool!"

CAR AND TRAVEL GAMES

Supplies: none

To make any car ride less tedious, here are some games to play:

- Don't Say That Word: Prohibit certain words from the conversation, such as "it," "no," or "yes," yet try to maintain a dialogue.
- Alphabet Signs: As you travel in a vehicle, see who can find the letters of the alphabet in order just by looking at signs along the journey.
- Are We There Yet? Each person guesses the time of arrival at various places along the route (for example, the next big city on the map or when you will stop for lunch or stop for gasoline).
- Animals: See who can spot the most cows or horses in the fields by the side of the road.
- Name That License Plate: Look for funny personal license plates that have names, initials, or unusual numerical combinations.

• Let's Find It: Agree to look for one special thing (for example, a covered bridge, a bright red car). The first one to spot that thing then chooses the next thing to look for.

CAT AND MOUSE

Supplies: none

One player is chosen to be the cat and another to be the mouse. The others form a circle and hold hands. The mouse is inside the circle, and the cat prowls around the outside.

The cat must try to break through the circle and catch the mouse, but the players in the circle do all they can to keep the cat out by raising or lowering their arms or standing close together. Despite all their efforts, the cat usually succeeds in ducking under their arms or forcing two players to let go of their hands. Then there is a furious chase around the inside of the circle.

Game Twist: Allow the mouse to run out of the circle when the cat gets in. The cat must then follow the mouse, who runs around the circle and ducks inside and then out again. The players, in this version of the game, are not permitted to try to stop the cat after he or she has succeeded in breaking into the circle.

CAT AND THE DOG

Supplies: 2 objects (any kind, see below)

Have students sit in a circle. You should also sit in the circle and hold two objects—for example, a pen and a book, or an apple and a sponge. You are Person One; pass one of the objects (such as the pen) to your right and say to that person:

Person One (to Person Two): "I found the cat."

Two (to One): "The what?"

One (to Two): "The cat."

Two hands the object to Three and says: "I found the cat."

Three (to Two): "The what?"

Two (to One): "The what?"

One (to Two): "The cat."
Two (to Three): "The cat."

Person Three passes the object to Person Four, and the same questions and answers continue, the questions being referred all the way back to you (Person One) each time.

As soon as the first object has been started, you'll start the second object (such as the book) around to your left saying, "I found the dog." That person answers as above. When the two objects cross in the center, both sets of questions must be repeated accurately back to you each time.

CATCH THE DRAGON'S TAIL

Supplies: handkerchief

Have students form groups of eight to 10 and have them line up, one behind the other. Everyone should put their arms on the waist or on the shoulder of the person in front of them. The last person in line tucks a handkerchief in the back of his or her pants with part of the handkerchief hanging out. At the signal, the "head" of the "dragon" (the front of the line) begins chasing its own "tail" (the end of the line), trying to snatch the handkerchief. The tricky part of this epic struggle is that the people at the front and the people at the end are clearly competing—but the folks at the middle aren't sure which way to go. Game ends when the head finally gets the handkerchief. Then the head dons the handkerchief and becomes the new tail, while the second person from the front becomes the new head.

Take it to the next level: Have two or more dragons trying to catch *each other's* tails.

CATEGORIES

Supplies: paper, pencils

This is undoubtedly one of the most entertaining pencil-and-paper games ever invented.

First, everyone agrees on a word containing five or six letters (longer words can be used if you wish). Next choose various categories, such as animals, flowers, vegetables, trees, cities, rivers, birds, actors, bands, movies, TV shows, colleges, musical instruments, sports, famous people, and so on.

Each player then makes a diagram on a piece of paper like the one shown here. The number of columns should be equal to the number of letters in the chosen word. The number of rows should equal the number of categories selected.

	G	A	M	E	S
ANIMALS	GNU		MULE	ELK	SLOTH
TREES		ASH		ELM	
CITIES	GRAND RAPIDS		MIAMI		ST. LOUIS
FLOWERS		ARBUTUS	MAY APPLE		SUN FLOWER

Suppose the chosen word is "Games." Everyone will write this in the diagram as shown, one letter at the head of each column. You would then say "Animals," and each player fills in as many columns as he can with the names of animals, each name beginning with the letter at the top of the column.

A player scores points for each name written down, plus additional points if no other players used the same name. For this reason, it is much better to choose unfamiliar words.

CHARADES

Supplies: slips of paper, pens or pencils, hat, watch or timer

The old game of charades is always a winner with small groups. Divide the group in half, and have each group write names of movies or TV shows on slips of paper for the other half to act out (one name on each slip). Mix up the papers in a hat. Then have one representative draw a name from the hat and give it to the other team, which will choose someone to act it out. Appoint a timekeeper for each team, and set a time limit of three minutes for each player.

Game Twist: Give each side a large drawing pad and a felt-tipped marking pen. One player from each team draws a movie or TV show without using any letters, numbers, or words. Then the player tries to get his or her team to guess the name by drawing. You can make this a faster-moving game by making two identical sets of about 10 titles and giving one set to each team.

You might have each player try to pantomime a particular occupation. Make up a list of creative suggestions, such as rock singer, astronaut, chimney sweep, or elephant trainer.

CHARIOT RACES

Supplies: masking tape, blankets, clean socks (if extras are needed)

This relay needs to be played on a smooth floor (like a polished gym floor). Set up a circular track and have teams line up at a starting line (you can use masking tape to set up boundaries and starting lines).

Have each team divide into groups of three. Each group has two horses and one rider. The "chariot" is a blanket pulled by the horses while the rider sits on the blanket, holding on to the corners of the blanket.

Have the students who are the horses wear only socks on their feet, and tell them they can't slip or slide at any time. Also tell them that the rider must never be in danger of coming off the "chariot" (blanket) because of the horses' speed or movement. This will require the horses to limit their speed, and will guarantee that groups won't go too fast during the relay, ensuring the rider's absolute safety. Each chariot must go around the track once, and then the next three players form a chariot, and so on. Teams can repeat the race to try to improve their times.

CHICKEN SHOOT

Supplies: Hula-Hoop, rubber chicken, balloon launcher

Shoot a rubber chicken out of a balloon launcher. Hold a Hula-Hoop at end of the room or field as the target.

Game Twist: Try Pig in a Blanket. Shoot a rubber pig up in the air with a balloon launcher. The students are divided into groups of four, each with a blanket. The teams of four attempt to catch the pig with a blanket held by the four team members.

(Games adapted from Jaroy Carpenter, *Get 'Em Pumped*, www.solidrockresources.com)

CLEARING CUSTOMS

Supplies: none

Fill an imaginary suitcase with items that begin with various letters of the alphabet. The students sit in a circle and the first player says, as though speaking to a customs agent, "I've been on vacation, and I'm only bringing back a _____ [naming any item]."

The next person in the circle now says the same phrase but also adds the name of an item that begins with the last letter of the previous item. Then the third person repeats the phrase, but he or she must say the previous item and then add another item that begins with the last letter of the second person's item. To keep it simple for the first couple of times through, limit the words to one syllable.

Here is an example:
Teenager 1: "I've been on vacation, and I'm only bringing back a cat."
Teenager 2: "I've been on vacation, and I'm only bringing back a cat and a tap."
Teenager 3: "I've been on vacation, and I'm only bringing back a tap and a pig."
Teenager 4: "I've been on vacation, and I'm only bringing back a pig and a gift."
Teenager 5: "I've been on vacation, and I'm only bringing back a gift and a torch."
Teenager 6: "I've been on vacation, and I'm only bringing back a torch and a hammock."

Game Twist: Make the game more challenging by allowing longer words. Or limit the words to certain categories like animals or food.

How to Be a Visible Leader

Make sure the crowd can see and hear the people who are leading a game. How many times has a student been about to suck pudding through a piece of new panty hose, but you couldn't see because someone was standing in the way? Never? Oh…maybe that's just happened to me.

But learn from my pain: If you're leading a game, step aside so everyone can see the action! If you're in a single-level room and the game you're leading is visual, elevate it somehow.

CLOTHESPIN FACE

Supplies: clothespins, watch or timer

Bring four students up front, each with a partner and a pile of clothespins in front of them. Students have 90 seconds to put the most clothespins all over their partner's faces (eyebrows, forehead, cheeks, ears, lips, and nose).

CLOTHESPIN HAIRSTYLES

Supplies: clothespins

Have students form teams of five to eight students. Give each team a whole bunch of clothespins. Have each team create a winning hairstyle out of clothespins. One of the team members provides the head of hair, and the other teammates decide on the hairstyle.

CLOTHES PINNING

Supplies: clothespins

Give everyone in the group six clothespins. At the signal each player tries to pin clothespins on other players' clothing. Each of a player's six pins must be hanging on six different players. Students must keep moving to avoid having clothespins pinned to them, while they try to hang pins on someone else. When students get rid of all six clothespins, they remain in the game but try to avoid having more pins stuck on them. They can't remove a clothespin once it has been pinned on them.

CLUMPS

 Supplies: none

Students mingle around the room, and you shout out a number. If the players hear "five," they must try to get into groups of five people and await further instruction. You'll then give the groups an assignment (for example: untie and tie everyone's shoes in the group; tell each other how they got here; stand in order of height). Then, after a few moments, call out a different group size and start another round.

Game Twist: Try Tin Pan Bang Bang, where no number is shouted. Instead, you bang on a stainless steel pot with a big metal spoon. The players must listen and count the number of bangs. If the leader stops banging on the pot after four bangs, then the players must get into groups of four.

(Game adapted from Wayne Rice and Mike Yaconelli, *Play It!*)

COFFEEPOT

Supplies: none

A player leaves the room while the others pick a secret verb, such as "kiss," "sniff," or "tickle." The player returns and tries to find out what the secret verb is by asking questions that may be answered only by "yes," "no," or "sometimes."

In each question, the guesser must substitute the words "coffeepot" for the verb. For example, the guesser might ask, "Do you coffeepot indoors?" or "Is it fun to coffeepot?" or "Is coffeepotting strenuous?" When the guesser has enough clues, he or she takes a guess at the verb. If the guesser is correct, the last person to answer a question leaves the room while the others think of a new verb. If the guesser is incorrect, the game continues until the guesser takes two more guesses. If the third guess is incorrect, the others tell the guesser the word, and the guesser may select the next player to leave the room.

COMMUNITY SNEEZE

Supplies: none

Have students form three groups. You'll ask the first group to say together "Hish" two or three times for practice; the second group "Hash"; and the third group "Hosh." You'll then ask the groups to add "ee"— that is, "hishee" for the first group, "hashee" for the second group, and "hoshee" for the third group. You'll then tell all three groups to say their words in unison. The ensuing sound is like an enormous sneeze. Smile and say, "Bless you!"

Take it to the next level: The first group can shout "ish," the second group "ash," the third "shoo" at the same time. This will also sound like a gigantic sneeze!

COMMUNITY TOSS

Supplies: ball (tennis or Nerf)

Have the students stand or sit in a circle about two feet apart from one another. The game is similar to Hot Potato, with a little bit of Concentration thrown in for fun. Have one person begin the game by tossing the ball to someone else in the circle. That person then throws it to another, and so on, until everyone has received and thrown the ball once. Players should toss the ball gently so others can catch it easily. If the ball is dropped, the group starts over. Eventually the last person throws the ball to the person who began the game. No one should get the ball a second time except the starter.

All players need to remember who threw the ball to them and who they threw the ball to. After doing this once, have players repeat the pattern, only faster. You may want to have someone time how long it takes to complete the pattern, and then try to beat that amount of time together.

Take it to the next level: After starting the ball in its pattern, add a second or third ball (or other unique object), following the same pattern. Or after starting the ball on its pattern, add a second ball on a *new* pattern at the same time.

COORDINATION CLAP

Supplies: none

Stand in front of the group, and extend your arms straight in front of you—one hand above your head and the other below your waist. Your palms should be facing each other. You will move your arms vertically in an up and down motion. Tell students that when you cross your hands over each other in front of your body, they are to clap their hands.

Slowly move your arms until your hands cross once (students will clap), then cross your hands again (students clap again). Now move your arms as if you're going to cross your hands, but stop just before they cross. Students will clap, anticipating the crossing of your hands. This causes much laughter.

Try the same thing a few more times, varying the number of times you really cross your hands before stopping just short. At the end of the game, cross your hands several times quickly and as students are clapping, say, "Thank you, thank you very much" and stop. This looks like everyone is applauding!

COTTON NOSE

Supplies: Vaseline, cotton balls, table, plates

Have students form groups of five to eight, and put Vaseline on the end of everyone's nose. Put a plate of cotton balls for each group on one end of a table, and put a second empty plate for each group at the other end.

On your mark, the first person in each group runs to the cotton balls, dips his or her nose into it, runs to the second plate, drops the cotton balls off without using hands, and then returns to the group. The next person repeats the process until the groups have emptied the first plate and filled the second.

(Game adapted from Jaroy Carpenter, *Get 'Em Pumped*, www. solidrockresources.com)

COUNT OFF!

Supplies: none

Tell all players that the object of this game is to close their eyes and see if they can count up to the number of players in the group with each player only saying one number once. Everyone should close their eyes, then begin. Someone just says "one" and then someone else says "two." If more than one person speaks at a time, you must start over with the number "one."

A CRIME HAS BEEN COMMITTED

Supplies: none

Gather your students and summarize a mysterious crime—the more bizarre, the better. For example, you might say, "Two girls went to the movies. When the movie was over, one girl was badly hurt, stuck through the back with something long, thin, and sharp. No weapon was found in her body."

Ask students to form teams of four to six. Team members should collaborate to form a reasonable explanation of the crime.

For instance, a team might report: "No one near the girls had a knife. The man behind the girl was holding a package of knitting needles he had bought for his wife. They dropped, and he picked then up. Holding the last one he had retrieved, he leaned over the front seat to watch a thrilling part of the movie; the girl also leaned forward. Then she suddenly sank back in her seat, overcome by the scene, and fell against the knitting needle. The man was frightened, pulled the needle free, and left the theater."

Consider the game ended when each team has shared a unique, creative explanation of the crime.

CROWS AND CRANES

Supplies: none

Divide the group into two teams. One side is the crows, the other the cranes. The two teams are lined up facing each other four or five feet apart. If you say, "crows," the crows must turn around and run, with the cranes in hot pursuit. You should prolong the first part of the word, as "cr-cr-rrrows," in order to keep both teams in suspense. You may also put the names of the teams into sentences, such as "I hear the sound of cr-cr-r-r-r-cracking and cr-cr-r-r-r-crunching. A cr-cr-r-r-r-cracker is being eaten by a big cr-r-r-r-crazy CROW." If any of the cranes succeed in touching a member (or members) of the crows before the crow crosses a given line (20 to 60 feet away), that player is considered a member of the cranes and must join the cranes when play continues.

CROWS AND CRAWDADS

Supplies: masking tape

Place a masking tape line down the middle of a long meeting area. Divide your group into two teams, and direct both to one end of the area. One team is called crows, the other crawdads. The object for each team is to get all members to the other end of the room (staying on their side of the line) from where they are standing. You'll give a command for how they'll travel, such as marching, baby steps, jumping jacks, or hopping on one foot. Then you'll say either the word "crows" or the word "crawdads." Only the team called must execute the command until the leader says stop.

DOG RACE

Supplies: none

Contestants are to run just as a dog does. Have them bend down so that the palms of their hands and the soles of their shoes are flat on the ground. They then advance; first, the right hand; second, the left foot; third, the left hand; and fourth, the right foot.

Now have students run any race you choose. At all times during the race, though, the players must keep the palms of their hands and the soles of their shoes flat against the floor.

DRAGON AND SPIDER

Supplies: none

The entire group, with the exception of one person, lines up in a single file, each one lightly holding on with both hands to the waist (or the shoulders) of the person in front.The entire line tries to ensnare the "spider," who is the lone individual not in the line. To catch the spider, the head and tail of the line must surround the spider and enclose that person in the circle.

Game Twist: Divide the group into teams of eight to 10 and have several spiders to catch.

DRAGON DODGE BALL

Supplies: ball

Have the entire group make a circle. Have four to five students form one team. This first team goes into the center of the circle and forms a line by placing their hands on the waist of the person in front of them. The people who make up the circle throw the ball at the "dragon," trying to hit the last person (must be below the waist). Once hit, the last person returns to the outside circle, and players continue to hit the new person at the end of the dragon until only one person is left and that person too is hit. A new team of four or five then goes into the middle.

(Game adapted from *The Ideas Library, Games 2*)

How to Keep Games Positive

The greatest thing you can do to keep games positive is to avoid eliminating players if at all possible. It seems incongruous to get players into groups to play a game, and then, after a brief period of participation, eliminate them one at a time from the activity. In many games, students are eliminated because they fail to give a "correct" response or performance. The players must often return to their chairs as observers and remain there until the conclusion of the game.

Being penalized for an incorrect response or some other failure and having to sit out the game is not fun and causes embarrassment. A game that puts teenagers on the sidelines may be returning them to the same self-conscious shell from which they may have momentarily emerged.

Instead of having students sit on the sidelines, your aim should be to keep students participating.

DROP THE KEYS

Supplies: set of keys, chairs

Have your group sit in chairs, forming a circle facing inward. Give the person who is "It" a set of keys, and have this person stand in the middle of the circle. (This person will not have a chair, so the circle is one chair short.) "It" will start by moving quickly around the inside of the circle grabbing the hand of someone of the opposite sex. The person whose hand is grabbed now grabs someone else's hand, again of the opposite sex. This will continue as students run around the circle (boy, girl, boy, girl). As the line gets longer, "It" can begin to go under arms and between people to get the line full of knots. While all this is happening, the person at the end of the line is trying to grab the hand of another person who is still sitting down. This becomes difficult because the line is knotting up. During this time, "It" is holding a set of keys. When "It" chooses, "It" drops the set of keys and runs to an empty chair. When others in the line notice the keys were dropped, they also dart for a chair. Whoever is left without a chair is the next person to be "It."

(Game adapted from *The Ideas Library, Games*)

ELBOW TAG

Supplies: none

Have players form pairs and scatter around a large room or area. One pair then volunteers to be "It." With partners' elbows linked together, all other pairs stand about 15 feet apart. All the players put their free hands on their hips, so the elbows jut out at an angle. One of the two players who are "It" now starts to chase the other. They run close to the others, weaving in and out among the pairs. At any time, the player who is being chased may hook onto the free elbow of any other player. When this happens, that chosen player's partner must free his or her elbow and run. That person is now the one being chased. If a player is tagged before linking onto someone's elbow, the tables are turned. The one who was being chased at once becomes the chaser.

Game Twist: Have two runners and two chasers. Or play the game with everyone lying on the floor next to a partner with their arms at their sides. At any point in the game, the person being chased can lie down next to somebody. When that happens, the person on the other side of the partner now has to get up and run.

ELECTRIC FENCE

Supplies: 2 poles, piece of rope or string

Have students form groups of eight to 10 students. Try to have the groups evenly divided according to height, age, and sex. Tie the rope between the two poles, beginning at about two feet off the floor.

The object of the game is for the entire group to get over the "electric fence" (the rope) without getting "electrocuted" (touching the rope). Each group takes a turn, with group members going one at a time. After each successful try, the rope is raised a little higher, as in regular high jump competition.

What makes this game interesting is that even though one player goes over the rope at a time, the other team members can help any way they want, even reaching back over the rope (without touching it). Once a person is over the fence, however, that player must stay over the fence and not come back around to help anyone. So the last person must somehow get over the fence without any help on one side. This game requires lots of teamwork and cooperation. Raise the rope a foot for each additional round.

How to Explain a Game Quickly

Get everyone's attention before demonstrating or explaining the game, and don't yell directions. Huddle players and groups together as close as is practical, and keep your demonstration or explanation quick and simple. Don't intellectualize a game; most questions are answered as teenagers are playing. You simply can't anticipate all possible game scenarios, so don't try to give an overly comprehensive explanation.

Make sure everyone understands the basic point or purpose of the game, and then get started. Your group wants to play, so detailed descriptions are futile. Describe in the fewest words possible what's to be done and what's to be avoided.

Don't be afraid to start a game even when a few teenagers are still confused. Youth leaders or fellow players can help these people along once you start.

ELEPHANT PANTOMIME

Supplies: none

Ask for three volunteers, and send them out of the room. Announce to the rest of the group that you are going to pantomime washing an elephant in front of the first volunteer. Now bring the first volunteer back into the room, and silently act out washing an elephant in front of the volunteer and the rest of the group. Don't let the volunteer know what you are doing; simply tell that person to pay close attention because he or she will act out the exact same thing for the second volunteer. After the first volunteer watches you do the pantomime, bring the second volunteer into the room and have the first volunteer do the elephant-washing pantomime (even though the first volunteer may not even know that it's supposed to *be* an elephant). Tell the first volunteer that it's OK to just try to imitate what you did.

Bring in the third volunteer, and have the second volunteer do the pantomime (as close as he can get it) for the third volunteer. The result is a lot of fun, because the pantomime keeps getting farther and farther away from the original. After all three are finished—and still without telling them for sure what they were acting out—start with the third volunteer and ask for a guess on what was being acted. If the third volunteer doesn't know, ask the second volunteer. If the second volunteer does not know, ask the first volunteer. If the first volunteer doesn't know, have the rest of the group tell all three of them.

Of course you may act out anything you want. However, if you choose the elephant-washing scene, include the following: Pull the elephant in on a rope. Dip a rag in a pail and wash the side of the elephant, jumping high to get all the way to the top. Crawl underneath and wash his belly and legs. Go to the front and wash his trunk, and wash the elephant's ears as well. At the end of the skit lift his tail up and, occasionally holding your nose, wash under his tail.

ELEPHANT STAMPEDE

Supplies: foam pool noodle and scissors (or 2 pieces of 18-inch foam pipe insulation)

The boundaries for the playing field must be clearly communicated to the group. Have one person be "It" (one elephant) for every 20 students. To make tusks for your elephant, cut a foam pool noodle in half, or cheaper still would be to use two pieces of foam pipe insulation, available at any hardware store. The person who is "It" holds one piece of the foam in each hand and chases people within the boundaries. "It" attempts to touch people below the waist with the foam pipe insulation. After someone is tagged, he or she holds hands with "It," and they each hold a piece of the foam in their outside free hands. Now they're both "It," and they chase after the other players. As new people are tagged and join the line of "It," the foam pieces are passed to the end of the line. The object is to be the last person tagged.

EMOTIONS

Supplies: paper, markers

Prepare signs by writing one-word emotions in large letters.

Examples: Sadness, Joy, Fear, Nervousness, Timidity, Weariness, Passion, Jealousy, Anxiety, Anger, Excitement, and Boredom.

Ask students to form pairs. Partners should sit on the floor and face each other (although one partner should face one end of the room and the other should face the opposite end of the room). Stand at one end of the room and hold up a sign with one emotion on it. The partners facing you will read the sign then describe their day yesterday in detail, incorporating the emotion into their description of their day. Body language is fine. They just can't use the actual word at all. Their partner attempts to guess the emotion. You then walk to the other end of the room and repeat the process with a new sign.

ENCORE

Supplies: none

Have students form teams of eight to 10 people. Shout out a word that is commonly found in songs (such as love, road, river, girl, baby, need, and so on). Each team must sing a song in unison using that word. Teams can't repeat a song. The game ends when none of the teams can come up with a new song.

ERECTOR SETS

Supplies: putty, toothpicks

Give each team of three to six students a ball of putty and a box of toothpicks. Tell each team to work together to design and build the best freestanding structure they can. Give all teams applause for being the tallest, the most structurally sound, the most original, the most creative, and so on.

Game Twist: Have students make *edible* erector sets with gumdrops and uncooked spaghetti.

How to Form Smaller Groups

Follow these do's and don'ts whenever you have your youth group form teams:

• Don't number off because students will place themselves in the line so that their numbers will be the same as their friends, and you'll end up with cliques.

• Don't assign teenagers to teams. If they lose the game, they might be tempted to blame you.

• Don't have team captains choosing players in front of the group.

• Do put different-colored candy jawbreakers into kids' mouths as they come into the room. When it's time to divide up, have them stick out their tongues. Blue tongues in one corner, red tongues in another corner, and so on.

• Do play the game Barnyard, where each young person who enters the room is given a piece of paper with the name of an animal that makes a noise (dog, cat, sheep, frog, for example). When it's time to form teams, turn off the lights. Then have the kids make their animals' noises and try to find others making the same sounds. Turn the light on and they're now in their teams.

• Do put them into groups according to the month of their birthdays. For instance, to create four groups, January through March birthdays in one corner, and so on.

• Do put them in teams alphabetically according to the first letter of their first or last name.

• Do divide them into two groups by odd- and even-numbered ages.

• Do have them fold arms over their chest. Those with right arm on top are on one team, lefties on the other.

• Do have them form groups according to their toilet paper choice (folding or scrunching).

GAMING TIP

EVERYBODY'S IT

Supplies: masking tape (or other markers if played outside)

This game is best played with shoes off. Have the boundaries for the playing area clearly marked or at least clearly understood by the participants. Have everyone spread out over the area or playing field. Give the start signal, and let the fun begin. Literally *everyone* is "It." The object is for everyone to tag as many people with their hands as they can without getting tagged themselves. When students are tagged, they aren't out but must put one of their hands on the place where they were tagged, and keep it there throughout the game. If they get tagged again, they must put their other hand on the place where they were tagged the second time. Since they now can't use either arm to tag, they can use their feet. When they get tagged the third time, they're out and must go outside the boundaries and wait until this round is over.

FASTEST STRAW IN THE WEST

Supplies: drinking straws

Give all the students a drinking straw, and have them put one end into their mouth. The idea is to see who can turn the straw around so that the other end of the straw is in his or her mouth—without using his or her hands. Students may only use their teeth, lips, mouth, and tongue.

FAVORITES

Supplies: none

Have students walk around as you yell out "favorite_____." You can choose anything—color, season, food, sport, fast-food restaurant, or comedy TV show. Then have students yell out their "favorite" of that category and get in groups according to their favorites. Then call out a new favorite.

Game Twist: Have students group with people of the same age, same birth month, same brand of shoes, same eye color, same grade in school, or same number of people in their immediate family.

FEETBALL

Supplies: chairs, ball

This is a good indoor game that is very active and requires teamwork. Divide the group into two teams, and seat them in two lines of chairs, facing each other. The object is for the teams to move a volleyball or similar ball toward and through their goal (at the end of the line) by using their feet only. Players must keep their arms behind the chairs to keep from touching the ball. To begin the game, drop the ball between the two teams in the middle. The game can be any length desired. To avoid injuries to feet, shoes should be removed. Also, make sure the two teams are just far enough apart that their feet barely touch when legs are extended on both sides.

How to Select Referees

As a rule of thumb, you'll need about one referee for every 20 teenagers. Pick referees who are fun, who enhance the game, and who understand that game "rules" are really only guidelines to make the game more enjoyable. Don't select referees who view themselves as authority figures whose main function is to strictly enforce the rules. Referees like this will find every type of minuscule mistake. They belong in the National Football League, not in your youth group.

Select referees who can help equalize lopsided scores in a game, so that if one team is desperately behind, the referees can become more observant of the other team.

You may want to have the referees wear striped jerseys or fluorescent jackets. And make sure they're familiar with the game so they don't have to keep referring to the game description.

FILL THE PITCHER

Supplies: water, large container (such as a salad bowl or bucket), smaller containers (such as pitchers or smaller buckets), drinking straws

Fill the large container with water. Have students form teams of six to eight students. The object of the game is to fill the smaller container with water to whatever the predetermined level is. Each team has one volunteer to be its small container holder. The volunteers' job is to line up across from their team, 30 to 50 feet away. Each volunteer must be sitting on the ground and holding the container on the top of his or her head. The rest of the participants will go one at a time to the large container, suck up a mouthful of water from the big bucket through the straw, hold the water in place, then run down to the smaller container and let the water out into the smaller container. Students do not have to spit any water back through the straw.

FIND THE LEADER

Supplies: none

Have students sit in a circle. Ask for a volunteer to be "It," and have this person leave the room. The remaining players should then select a leader. When "It" is called into the center of the circle, the leader slyly starts some motion, such as waving a hand, making a face, wiggling fingers, clapping hands, or lifting one foot up and down. Everyone should immediately imitate the leader, who changes the motions frequently. "It" tries to guess who the leader is. When the leader is discovered, another volunteer becomes "It."

FINGER BALANCE

Supplies: foam pipe insulation

See who can balance a piece of foam pipe insulation tubing on one finger for the longest time. Expand this simple, fun game in any creative way you want!

FINGERS UP

Supplies: none

This is my favorite pairs game. Have students form pairs and face their partner with their hands behind their back. On your count of three, have students bring out both hands in front of their face so that their partners can see their hands. Each person should hold up as many fingers on each hand as he or she chooses. This is a fun game between the partners, not with anyone else in the room. The object is to be the first of the pair to say the total number of fingers being held by all four hands. (A closed fist means zero fingers.)

Tell students that there's a secret to the game. The secret is to count the number of fingers you're going to hold up before you bring your hands out from behind your back. Then you just have to add the number of fingers that your partner is holding up to the total you're holding up. Play three rounds of this game.

FLAMINGO FOOTBALL

Supplies: football

Announce that you are going to play "tackle football, boys against the girls!" The boys usually get pretty charged up about that idea. Then announce that the rules are the same as regular tackle football, except the boys must hold one foot off the ground with one hand at all times. They must run, pass, hike, and catch—on one foot.

(Game adapted from Wayne Rice and Mike Yaconelli, *Play It!*)

FORTUNATELY/UNFORTUNATELY

Supplies: none

Have each student find a partner. Partners should face each other, and one person begins a sentence with the word *fortunately*. (For example, "Fortunately the weather is sunny today.") That person's partner then continues the conversation with a sentence starting with the word *unfortunately*. (For example, "Unfortunately it will probably rain tomorrow.") The first person then starts a sentence with "fortunately," and they go back and forth until one of them runs out of things to say or there is a pause of more then three seconds.

FOUR ON A COUCH

Supplies: couch (or 4 chairs), paper, pen or pencils, hat

Have students form two easily identified teams (for example, one team is wearing mostly a certain color, or has hats or sunglasses).

Have everyone sit in a circle with no one on the couch (or four chairs if you don't have a couch). The object of the game is to get all of one's team on the couch at the same time.

Everyone writes their name on a slip of paper and puts it in a hat; names are jumbled up and each person pulls a name out of the hat. But if students pull their own name out, they must put it back and draw another. It's extremely important that once names are drawn, no one says whose name they have!

Have the person to the left of the couch call out any name within the group; whoever drew that name will get up and take a spot on the couch. The next person calls out another name, and so on, until all four spots on the couch are taken. If the four on the couch are not on the same original team, then the next person calls out another name and the person who has that name takes the very first person's place on the couch.

Everyone takes a turn and says a name, hoping the name he or she calls belongs to someone on the team. Students will have to remember who has whose name in order to get four from their team on the couch at the same time. One rule: The same name can't be called twice in a row.

(Game adapted from *The Ideas Library, Games 2*)

Game Twist: The goal of the game could be for the boys to get four boys on the couch and the girls to get four girls on the couch.

FREEZE FRAME

Supplies: paper, pen

Have students form small groups of three to five. Give groups pieces of paper on which you've written specific poses. Some example poses include: someone seeing a mouse; a minister delivering a sermon; a baseball player protesting a decision. Give each group 30 seconds to come up with a pose, then have them assume the pose for the rest of the group.

Game Twist: Try Biblical Freeze Frame. Example poses include: the baptism of Jesus, Jesus stills the sea, the Last Supper, Abraham attempts to sacrifice Isaac, Daniel in the lions' den, the story of David and Goliath, the feeding of 5,000, the giving of the Law, the good Samaritan, Jonah and the big fish, the parting of the Red Sea, the wise men bearing gifts, and Samson pulling down walls.

How to Get Students to Participate

Encourage participation in games, but don't force it. We can't force our students to play. Remember that the goal of any game is to build students up, not tear them down. One person's fun should never be at someone else's expense. Embarrassing kids in front of their peers can have deep and hurtful repercussions—just the opposite of what we hope will happen in teenagers' lives.

Some students think they aren't good enough to play. They are afraid of ridicule and embarrassment. Some students may feel uncoordinated or unskilled. Some students have had negative experiences playing games in the past. Allow students to observe as long as they're not disturbing those who are participating.

Encourage timid students to take risks. No type of player needs more sympathetic or tactful understanding and help from you than the shy. Some students suffer greatly through their shyness. They should first be brought into play in some form of game that does not make them conspicuous; one, for instance, in which they do what all the other players do. Encourage them with praise of their successful efforts, and special care should be taken not to call attention to their failures. One bit of caution: You may express an extra quotient of praise for a student's efforts, but you should be careful not to overdo it. Too much praise may achieve just the opposite of the intended effect, and the student could be perceived as being a "teacher's pet." This can be social suicide for some teenagers.

FRUIT BASKET

Supplies: paper, pen

This is a fast action game. Have students sit in a circle, except for the player chosen to be "It," with every seat taken. Ask each student to say the name of a fruit. Write each fruit name down on a piece of paper. Everyone should choose a different fruit. The player who is "It" will stand in the center of the circle. Name two or more fruits such as "apple and pineapple," and have the student who chose "apple" and the student who chose "pineapple" quickly exchange seats. "It" will try to get an empty seat in the scramble. The next "It" can be another volunteer or the person left without a chair.

Any combinations of fruits may be given. If you call out "Fruit basket upset," everyone must exchange seats.

Game Twist: Have the group count off by fours as they are sitting in the circle. All the number one's are lemons, number two's oranges, number three's apples, and number four's bananas. If you say "bananas and oranges," then all bananas and oranges quickly exchange seats. "It" tries to get a seat in the scramble. Or you may play Flower Garden, where the players are given the names of flowers and the term for everyone to change chairs is "Poison Ivy."

In Mailman, the players are given names of cities, and the name for all to change chairs is "Next Day Air."

How to Have Leaders (Including You!) Join a Game

Hopefully the youth leaders in your ministry are there to hang out with kids, not to just be chaperones. Chaperones often view their jobs as merely keeping "super brat" in line and the couples apart. Pure chaperones aren't fun, and no kid wants a relationship with one. Therefore, the youth leaders in your ministry should be in the groups with the students and participate as much as possible.

As the leader, you should occasionally get into the game yourself as well. It is not necessary or advisable to be in the center of play with the group all of the time, but it is a mistake not to play at all. By taking part in the game, you can encourage and energize the group. Then you can drop out, and the group will more or less go forward on its own momentum. You can also take part by joining a weaker or more timid group.

Nothing can more quickly gain the respect and affection of teenagers than joining in a game with them. One of the most valuable side benefits of playing in games with your students is to produce a more natural relationship.

GARGLE A TUNE

Supplies: drinking glasses, water, paper, pen

Write songs that will be familiar to students on pieces of paper. Hand students glasses of water. Then, one at a time, show the name of a song only to the person (or several people, if you have a few students "performing" at the same time) doing the gargling. Have the person (or people) take a sip of water and attempt to gargle the tune. The rest of the students in the room should be listening closely so they can guess the song. Be ready for water through the nose! Continue with other students and other songs.

GELATIN BLOW

Supplies: 4-foot-long piece of transparent ¾-inch surgical tubing (hardware stores have this), gelatin mix, water

Put a small amount (about 2 tablespoons) of watered-down colored gelatin inside the tubing. Have two students on opposite ends of the tubing blow into the tubing until the gelatin blows out; one person will swallow it—or get it all over the face!

GELATIN SUCK

Supplies: drinking straws, bowls, gelatin

It's as easy as it sounds. Ask for volunteers to come forward. You can give them each a straw and a bowl of liquefied gelatin. See how fast students can suck it all up!

GET THE STICK

Supplies: sticks (such as plastic tent stakes)

Place several sticks in a line at one end of the playing field. Make sure there are fewer sticks than students. Have students line up across a designated line, about 40 yards away from the sticks. Have students lie down flat on their backs, with their heads pointing in the direction of the sticks at the other end of the playing field. Signal them to get up and begin racing for the sticks at the other end. Have the participants line up again, remove several sticks, and continue the game while those who didn't get sticks watch and cheer the others on.

GOING TO PISMO BEACH

Supplies: none

With the players seated in a circle, announce, "I am going to Pismo Beach and will take my _____." Here you name some item, such as a dog, airplane, taco, CD, or bushel of potatoes. The second player immediately continues, "I am going to Pismo Beach and will take my _____," naming another item. All the other players, in turn, repeat the statement and name something different.

When the first round has been completed, begin the second round, this time telling what you will do with whatever you intend to take. If you said a dog in the first round you might say, "I am going to wash my dog." The other players in turn repeat the same sentence, except that each substitutes for *dog* the name of the thing that they mentioned in the first round. So the statements might include, "I am going to wash my bushel of potatoes," "I am going to wash my CD," and so on. (Make sure these stay appropriate; if not, stop and either move to another game, or begin the round anew.)

When the second round is finished, the third round begins, this time with the second player. This student tells of something that he will do with whatever he had selected from the first round, and the others repeat his statement, of course substituting the specific items they are taking to Pismo Beach. The game continues until each player has begun a round.

GO-TAG

Supplies: none

Everyone kneels in a line, alternate players facing opposite directions. If you think of the line as the central axis, you can imagine an oval track running around the line. (There's no need to mark boundaries; the track is defined by the axis.) The student at one end of the line will be the first runner. This student may run around the track in either direction throughout the game. The student at the other end will be the chaser. This student may start running either clockwise or counterclockwise, but may not switch directions once starting. The object of the game is for the chaser to tag the runner.

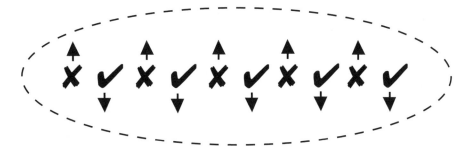

The chaser works with the other people kneeling in the line. As the chaser is chasing around the track, the chaser can tap the back of any kneeling player and shout, "Go!" The tapped player steps forward to begin the chase, while the old chaser replaces that player, kneeling in the line. This maneuver makes the chaser able to cross over the center of the line and change the direction of the chase.

The key to this game is to change chasers frequently and rapidly enough to catch the runner off guard. Running speed is not as important as reflexes and quick thinking.

When the runner is tagged, that student kneels at one end of the line, the person who tagged him becomes the new runner, and the person at the other end of the line becomes the starting chaser for the next round.

GROUP IMPRESSIONS

Supplies: none

Have students form two groups. Tell the groups what scene is to be acted out by both teams at the same time. Some examples might include:

- scariest part of a movie,
- a gut-wrenching song (listening to or giving),
- you have gotten food poisoning and are dying,
- teenagers at a rock concert,
- room full of laughing gas, or
- you just discover you are naked.

After giving the scene, say "go," and both groups act it out at the same time. Encourage students to keep impressions going for 10 seconds.

These scenarios create lots of noise and laughter. They're fun and require no acting ability!

Game Twist: Tell the group to imitate an animal sound—for example, a dog, frog, cow, or sheep.

GUESS THAT SMILE

Supplies: video camera, TV/VCR, paper, pen

Set up a video camera wherever students enter your meeting room. Have everyone who walks by the camera look in it and "smile!"

Have your camera operator be sure that the only thing appearing in the video is the students' smiles, *not* their faces. Also have someone write down the students' names in order. You'll need this list so that you will know who's who!

Play the video for students sometime during your time together. Pause after every smile, and let them guess whose "purty smile" they are viewing!

HA-HA-HA GAME

Supplies: none

This game works best with all the girls in one group and all the boys in another group. One person lies down on the floor (on his or her back). One by one, the rest of the students lie down with their heads on the stomach of the person who lay down before them.

After everyone is down on the floor, the first person says, "Ha," and the second person says, "Ha Ha," while the third says, "Ha Ha Ha," and so on.

Put on a serious face, and tell your students that if anyone goofs up and laughs, everyone must start over. But it will be hard to be serious because as a person says "ha…" the stomach moves, as does the person's head that is resting on it.

HASTY SPEECH

Supplies: none

I usually don't like these kind of word games, but this is kind of fun, and brief! "A farmer had 20 sick sheep and one died. How many were left?" The answer is 19 (not 25).

HIP CHARADES

Supplies: slips of paper, bag, pens

This game is a lot of fun. However, if you don't think it's appropriate for your group, modify it any way you'd like. (You might want to play it with a smaller group of mature students.) Have your students form two teams. Write any words on slips of paper and put the papers into a bag. Have volunteers from each team take slips out of the bag and spell the word for their team members by moving their hips (spelling the words with their behinds). Make sure they do not say any words to give away clues. If their team does not figure out the word after two spellings, the other team gets to guess.

HORSEY-BACK TAG

Supplies: tape

Teams consist of two partners—one horse and one rider. The horse should place two pieces of tape on the rider's back. The tape should be easily seen and reached by the other riders.

The riders should then get on the backs of the horses with their arms wrapped around the horse's neck (piggyback style). When the signal is given, the horses carry the riders around the playing field, and the riders try to steal the pieces of tape from other riders without getting their own tape stolen.

(Game adapted from *The Ideas Library, Games 2*)

HOSE-HEAD

Supplies: tennis ball, nylon hose (thigh high or just cut the legs from a pair of pantyhose), safety goggles

Have students form pairs. Put a tennis ball in the end of each stocking, all the way at the toe end. Have the students put the stocking over their head and face (with the ball dangling in front). Then have them bend over and start swinging their stocking and ball. They should try to use their swinging hose to catch the other swinging hose and pull it off their partner's head without using their hands. It becomes a tug-of-war of stockings. Give eye protection such as safety goggles to all participants.

Game Twist: Put a handful of flour instead of a tennis ball in each pantyhose.

HOUND AND RABBIT

Supplies: none

Have your students form groups of three, with two of the students holding hands and the third one in the middle. Tell the two they are forming a hollow tree. The student inside the tree is the rabbit. There should be one more rabbit than the number of trees. One student should also be the hound.

The hound chases the odd-numbered rabbit, who may take refuge in any tree at any time by running under the arms of the players forming the hollow trees. But no two rabbits may lodge in the same tree, so as soon as a hunted rabbit enters a tree (by going under the connected arms/branches of the trees), the rabbit already there must run for another tree. Trees stay "rooted" and can't move. Whenever the hound tags a rabbit, they switch roles.

Game Twist: Have an extra rabbit for the hound to chase. Or form each tree with three players and one rabbit inside.

HOW IS IT LIKE ME?

Supplies: various objects (see game description)

Send a volunteer out of the room, then have the group select an object, such as a chair. The volunteer returns and asks the other students, "How is it like me?" Everyone should answer truthfully, such as "It stands upright," "It has a nice back," "It is supportive," and so on. The volunteer has three guesses to discover what the object is. Continue with more volunteers and objects.

HULA-HOOP PASS

Supplies: Hula-Hoop

Have students stand in a circle holding hands, with one Hula-Hoop between two of the hands. The object is to pass the hoop all the way around the circle without letting go of any hands.

Take it to the next level: Use two Hula-Hoops going in opposite directions. (Hula-Hoops are available at department and discount stores for only a few dollars each. You can also use 6- to 8-foot long loops of webbing.)

HUMAN FOOSBALL

Supplies: string or cord, chairs, ball

Foosball is a table version of soccer. Human Foosball imitates the table game on a larger scale. Divide a playing field into 10 sections using string or cord strung across the field about waist high and attaching it at both ends to folding chairs. Each team should have 10 players (this can be adjusted) placed in the pattern of the table game.

The object of the game is to kick the ball into the other team's goal. The ball may be advanced using any part of the body except the hands and arms. This rule also applies to the goalie. Players may only advance the ball while it is in their sections and may move laterally as much as they like. Have spotters on the edges whose job is to roll the ball back into play once it has been kicked out of bounds.

Develop a rotation system so that everyone can play the different positions. Use any round ball (a soccer ball works best).

ICE CHEST

Supplies: XXXL T-shirts, coolers, ice, scooper

Beforehand, have the boys remove their shirts and change into the XXXL T-shirts.

Make sure they tuck the shirts in really well. Have each of the boys stand by a cooler of ice (20 to 40 pounds per cooler), and give the girls a large scooper. When you say "Go!" the girls will begin shoveling the ice into the boys' T-shirts. Give the 10-second warning after a minute or two, depending on the crowd's interest.

(Game adapted from Jonathan McKee's Web site, *www.thesource4ym.com*)

IDENTICAL SIT DOWN

Supplies: none

Have your students form pairs with someone of equal size, and have them stand back to back, with heels and heads touching and arms folded across chests. Have them try to lower themselves to a sitting position on the floor by bending their knees and moving their feet slowly out in front of them. Their shoulders and heads must always touch each other, and they must keep their arms folded. They must try to sit down on the floor with their legs extended in front of them.

IF...MOVE...

Supplies: chairs

Have each player sit in a chair with the chairs in a circle. You begin by saying a series of "If you _____ (a descriptive phrase) _____ move _____ (between 1 & 5) _____ chairs to the _____ (right or left) _____."

Example: "If you got up on the left side of your bed this morning move three chairs to your left." When students move, they may find someone already sitting in their new chair. If so, they are instructed to sit carefully on that person's lap. The piles will grow. More examples may include: "If you are wearing green," or "If you are in eighth grade," or "If your birthday is this month."

I HAVE NEVER...

Supplies: pennies (or pinto or jelly beans)

This game works best with five to 15 players. Give each player an equal number of pennies (or pinto beans or jelly beans), equal to the number of overall participants (if there are 15 players, everyone needs 15 pieces).

Have students sit in a circle. Go around the circle and complete the sentence, "I have never _____(fill in a true statement about you)_____. "Every person should select something he or she suspects other people in the group have done.

If other players have done the thing named, they must give the person making the statement one of their pennies. This is a great way to learn interesting facts about people! To keep the game interesting and avoid boring or embarrassing anyone, tell the students not to share geographical situations ("I have never been north of Oregon") or inappropriate items ("I have never done drugs").

IN COMMON

Supplies: none

Have your students form pairs, and have each pair find five unusual things they have in common. Ask each pair to prepare statements about things they have in common. Two of the statements should be false, and one should be true. Give each pair a chance to share its three statements, and have the rest of the group attempt to guess what thing the partners have in common.

INNER TUBE AMOEBA

Supplies: 27-inch bicycle inner tubes

Have your students form groups of eight to 10, and have the groups bunch up together as closely as they can. Have each group slowly slide an inner tube over all group members' heads, pulling it down around all the group members' waists. Then have them try to take two steps to the left—or move around some obstacles. They must work together to get anywhere. It's a riot for everybody! Afterward, have them slowly pull the inner tube back over their heads.

Take it to the next level: See how many students you can get into an inner tube without it breaking. (I have had as many as 58 in one 27-inch inner tube.) Or during the summer months, play Sitting Ducks, where students get in groups of eight to 10 inside the 27-inch bicycle inner tubes at one end of a football field. At the opposite end, students use water balloon launchers to attempt to splatter them with water balloons.

JELLY BEAN TRADE

Supplies: multicolored jelly beans

Everyone is handed 10 jelly beans (all different colors). Students try to get 10 of one color by trading with other people, one jelly bean at a time.

JENKINS SAYS

Supplies: table, chairs, quarter

Have students form two even teams (about four to eight students per team), who sit along a fairly long table facing each other. Each team should choose a leader and have that person sit in the center of the line of players, so the leaders face each other. One team is given a quarter. All the players on that team put their hands under the table and move the quarter from hand to hand so the other team won't know where the quarter is.

The leader of the team without the quarter calls, "Jenkins says hands up," and all the other team members' hands come up, with palms outward toward the guessing party, fingers closed down tightly over the palms, the coin hidden in one of the hands.

The other team may look at the hands from their side of the table in this way as long as they choose. You will then say, "Jenkins says hands down," and all the hands fall, palms downward, simultaneously flat on the table. All try to make as much noise as possible in slamming their hands down, so as to drown the clink of the coin as it strikes the table.

The other side now tries to guess whose hand the coin is not under. Only the leader of this side can give the orders to the side holding the quarter. The leader directs the players who his team thinks does *not* have the quarter to take their hands off. Should the leader make a mistake and call up a hand under which the coin is hidden, the coin remains with the same side, and the number of hands still on the table counts for that side. But if the last hand left on the table covers the quarter, it then goes to the other team.

JUMP-ROPE CHALLENGES

Supplies: rope

Have students form groups of about eight to 15 students and have two volunteers from each team grab an end of a long rope and begin to twirl it. Have the rest of their group attempt to run through it as it is twirling.

Take it to the next level: Have group members run through the rope but take one jump as they do so. Or see how many people you can get jumping in the rope at one time. Start slow and add people.

KAZOO ORCHESTRA

Supplies: kazoos

A kazoo is a small hollow instrument that is played by humming or singing through it. Provide each player with one kazoo. Divide the group into two teams. Each team forms a kazoo band, decides on a tune, and plays it for everyone else!

KITE-FLYING TO THE EXTREME

Supplies: kites

Here are several activities to do with kites:
- Altitude—Everyone has 100 yards of string and sees how high they can get their kite to go.
- Looping—Everyone has 50 yards of string and sees how many times they can make their kite loop.
- Reeling In—Once all kites are out on 50 yards of string, a signal is given and everyone reels in, winding the string around a single stick and seeing how fast they can wind in all the string.

Pay special attention to:
- Manner of flying and behavior in the air.
- Workmanship and neatness in building a homemade kite.
- Artistry, style, coloring, and beauty in building a homemade kite.

Game Twist: Have students form two teams who take turns shooting kites out of the air with rubber balls or water balloons.

LAP CIRCLE

Supplies: none

The students stand in a tight circle, all facing the same direction. The tighter the circle, the more likely they are of success. Instruct them—all at the same time—to sit down on the lap of the person behind them. It helps to give a count of three. On "one" they bend their knees. On "two" they touch the knees of the person behind them with their behinds. On "three" they put all their weight on the knees of the person behind them. Have everyone try to take three steps while sitting on each other's laps.

LARD SCULPTING

Supplies: lard (or fat or Crisco)

Go to the store and purchase a large quantity of lard. Place it on a table in one massive pile (the larger the pile, the more impressive). Separate the pile into several smaller piles. Give students two minutes to make the perfect sculpture. Allow other students to award the sculptures on creativity, originality, craftsmanship, and innovation.

Game Twist: Try Sculpturnary (similar to Pictionary) using modeling clay. Instead of drawing, use the clay to make the objects. Have students form groups, and have one volunteer from each group sculpt the same object. Each group attempts to guess the created object. The only rules are: no letters or numbers, and no charades.

How to Handle Challenging Students

Avoid embarrassing students. No one has the right to humiliate a student before his friends. Students who are over-excitable players, disruptive players, or cheating players need special attention. In most cases, the disruptive and over-excitable players are so gripped by the enthusiasm of the moment that they are not really aware of what they are doing. You, by smoothly moving into another type of game—perhaps a quieter, calmer one—can soothe injured feelings and settle raucous emotions.

If cheating or unfair play occurs during a game, quietly point out that there has been an infraction of the rules and continue. (If points are involved, award points to the student or team against which the offense was made.) If a student continues to cheat, you should privately talk with the student. The student should not be called out in the middle of the game and be made an object of attention. A short break between games usually affords a moment or two for personal conversation.

LEG CRAWL

Supplies: none

Get your group into teams with the same number of students in each team (anywhere from five to 15). Arrange the teams in parallel lines 10 feet apart. The first player of each team steps forward and spreads his or her feet. Immediately the second player crawls through the first player's legs and rises close in front of him with feet spread. The third player in the column crawls through the legs of the first two, coming up in front of the second player. The others follow in succession. As the players come up from between each other's legs and stand in closed columns, each should hold the waist of the player in front. They continue doing this until they reach a goal line about 50 feet away.

LOOK OUT FOR THE BEAR

Supplies: none

One student is chosen to be the "bear," and he hides in some part of the building or field. The rest of the students, with their backs turned, are standing at the goal.

As soon as the students have counted to 50, they all scatter and hunt for the "bear." The student who finds him first calls out, "Look out for the bear," and all the students run to the goal.

If the bear catches anyone while running for the goal, they become "bears." These "bears" hide together and the game continues until all the students are "bears."

MAD ADS

Supplies: several copies of the same magazine

Ahead of time, make a list of about 30 or 40 advertisements throughout the magazine (big ads and small ads).

Have your students form two or four teams, and give each team the same issue of a magazine. Have the teams pick a runner for their team.

Instruct the teams to tear the pages out of the magazine and divide them up between the team members before the game begins. They can spread them out on the floor if they want. Stand an equal distance from all the teams, and call out the name of an advertisement. The objective is to locate the advertisement, hand it to the runner, and get it to you.

(Game adapted from Wayne Rice and Mike Yaconelli, *Play It!*)

MAKING RAIN

Supplies: chairs

Divide the students sitting in chairs into four sections. Point at each group beginning with group one (then two, three, and four), and tell that section what motion to make when you point to it. Students are to continue making that motion until you return to their section and stop the motion.
- Motion one—Rubbing hands together
- Motion two—Snapping fingers, alternating hands
- Motion three—Patting thighs, alternating hands
- Motion four—Stomping feet

The noise created sounds like a light rain in the beginning and builds to a thunderstorm. As you point to each group the second time—beginning with section four, then three, then two, then one—the storm will dissipate.

MATTRESS RELAY

Supplies: twin mattress

The group is divided into two teams. The boys lie flat on their backs on the floor, side by side, alternating head to foot.

One girl is transported over the line of boys on a single mattress and jumps off at the end. The mattress is then passed back, and another girl gets on. If any girl falls off, she must get back on the mattress where she fell off. The object is for the team of boys to transport the girls quickly. This works best when the boys are older teenagers. Have spotters along each side of the path.

MINI MARSHMALLOW LAUNCHERS

Supplies: mini marshmallows, half-inch PVC pipe (available at any local hardware store), large paper cups

For this game you'll need to have students make mini marshmallow launchers made from sections of half-inch PVC pipe. No glue is required.

Place a miniature marshmallow in one end of the PVC pipe (the drier the marshmallow, the better—it'll stick to the pipe if wet). Take a deep breath then place your mouth on the pipe and blow the marshmallow out the other end. One game suggestion is to aim the launcher at a 45-degree angle and blow a marshmallow high in a huge arc. Have students try to catch it in large paper cups. Do not aim at people's faces. Do not put the pipe in your mouth and then take a breath of air, because the marshmallow will come back into your mouth and throat.

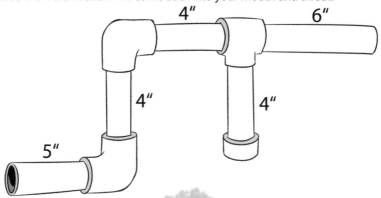

How (and Why) to Stop a Game at Its Peak

When a game is played casually around a picnic table or while driving in a car, no one has to tell the players when to stop. When it is a larger group of people and in a more organized setting, it is sometimes necessary for you to bring the game to a halt. If you don't, the game may become dull, with players dropping out because of sheer boredom. "Kill" a game before it dies on its own. You should be alert to the level of interest of the group. It is better to stop a game while the group is still actively enjoying it, so that their enthusiasm will be carried over to the next activity. Usually, the best way to end a game is to suggest that another be played.

Games have a fun quotient that's similar to a bell curve. They start out in neutral and begin to build. Every game has a peak. Don't go beyond this point. No matter how much fun kids are having, stop the game when they're having the most fun. They may want to continue playing the game, but don't let them. What they'll remember about the game is the last 20 seconds (when they were having so much fun), and if you decide to play it again in a few weeks, they'll be thrilled.

Don't let the game fizzle out. If you let it go on past the peak, the game begins to get stale, and kids won't want to play it again. You can tell a game has passed its peak when students' attentions begin to wander, students modify the rules on their own, students intentionally break the rules, or students stop playing.

MINISTER'S CAT

Supplies: none

The first player says, "The minister's cat is an active cat." The next player says the same, substituting the word "active" with some other word beginning with the same letter. The sentence goes around the circle with a different adjective for the cat by each player, all starting with the letter "a," until someone can't think of a word and starts with "b" and so on through the whole alphabet.

MIXED-UP FEATURES

Supplies: none

The players sit or stand in a circle with "It" in the center. "It" approaches one of the players, touches his or her own nose, and says, "This is my ear." As "It" counts to seven, the other player must answer in reverse, touching his or her ear and saying, "This is my nose."

"It" continues with other people in the circle in a similar fashion, pointing to various parts but calling each by the name of some other part. If the player does not answer correctly before "It" counts to seven, that player becomes "It" for the next round.

MOTHER CAREY'S CHICKENS

Supplies: none

Students get in lines of about five people with both hands on the waist of the person in front them. These are the chickens. One student who is not in any line is the fox. Mother Carey is at the head of each line and, with arms extended, swings the line about to keep the fox from tagging the last chicken. As soon as the fox tags the last chicken of a line, the players line up again with new chickens, Mother Carey, and fox.

Game Twist: Have more than one fox.

MOVIE CLIPS

Supplies: TV, VCR/DVD player, movies

Have several videos or DVDs cued beforehand. Play two to four seconds of a movie clip and have students guess what movie it's from.

Game Twist: Have students complete the next line in the movie. Or play this game using a song instead of a movie.

MRS. MUMBLE

Supplies: none

Have your students sit in a circle. Everyone should have their teeth covered with their lips. The first student turns to a second student and asks, "Does Mrs. Mumble have any vegetables?" The second student—also with teeth covered—replies, "I think she has _____ [names a vegetable]; I'll have to ask my neighbor" and turns to the third player and repeats the first question. The third player repeats the answer with a new vegetable. Students can't repeat a vegetable and can't reveal their teeth. Students will definitely start laughing at how silly they sound.

NAME GAME

Supplies: none

Have your students form two or more teams. Start with a name of a person (example: Julia Roberts). The other team must come up with another name starting with the last letter of the last name (example: Sean Connery). The names can be people living or dead.

Game Twist: Do the same game but with song titles instead of names of people.

NEWSPAPER RACE

Supplies: newspaper

Each student is given two pieces of newspaper, one for each foot. Students place one piece of newspaper in front of them and step on it with their right foot. They then place the other piece of newspaper for their left foot and so on, being allowed to step only on newspaper. Students race to a given spot using the pieces of newspaper and then return without using the newspaper.

Take it to the next level: Give each student two pie pans instead of pieces of newspaper.

NYLON HOSE GAMES

Supplies: nylon hose (see below for specific games)

The following games involving nylon hose originated in the book *Brite-Tite Book O' Fun* by Glenn Q. Bannerman (professor emeritus recreation and outdoor ministries), Beth Bannerman Gunn, and Lee Ann Bannerman.

• Nylon Hose Ball and Rocket

Gather white nylon hose for stuffing. Use one nylon hose for a golf ball–size ball, five nylon hose for a softball size, and eight nylon hose for a larger ball. Roll white nylon hose into a ball, keeping one end loose. Pull the loose end of the nylon hose over the stuffing to maintain a ball shape. Put this ball into the thin end of a separate nylon hose. On the side of the ball where the nylon hose length continues, tie an overhand knot. Be sure the knot is tight and as close to the ball as possible. Reach into the nylon hose, grasp the ball, and pull it through, turning the nylon hose inside out. Stretch the outer nylon hose so it's taut, and mold the ball shape with hands. Grasp the nylon hose close to the ball, and twist tightly to smooth the "skin." Tie an overhand knot firmly against the ball. Repeat previous four steps four times. To make a ball, cut off the excess nylon hose. To make a rocket, leave excess nylon hose as it is or fringe it several inches from the knot.

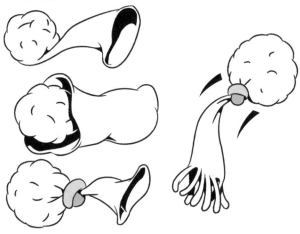

• Nylon Hose Doughnut

Cut two 1-inch strips from thick elastic nylon hose scraps. Set these aside for later use. Pull the thick elastic end of a nylon hose up over the elbow of one arm, letting the excess hang from your hand. Fold over the top edge of the nylon hose, and then roll it down your arm. When the roll reaches your wrist, pull it up your arm and roll it down again. The tighter you pull and roll, the more solid your doughnut will be. When you reach the end of your nylon hose, roll the doughnut off your arm. Roll the doughnut until the thin end of the nylon hose is even all around. Take the strips you cut earlier, and cut them each into two loops to make four strips or ties. Tie the strips around the nylon hose doughnut to keep the edge from unrolling.

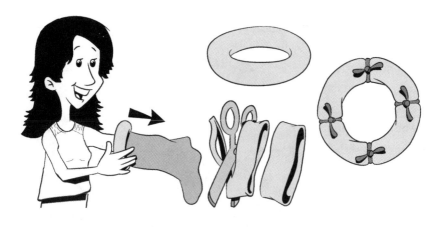

• Nylon Hose Flying Disc

Arrange six nylon hose doughnuts around a central doughnut so all the seams are facing up. You'll need to use doughnuts that haven't yet been tied with nylon hose ties. Cut six 2-inch sections of a nylon hose to make six loops. Stretch the loops, and then cut them in half to make 12 ties. Tie the six doughnuts to the center doughnut. Tie the six doughnuts to each other. Finally, tie the outside edge of each doughnut so the seam won't unravel. The ties may be trimmed close to the knot or left long.

• Creating a Small Nylon Hose Geode Ball

You will need one flying disc, a round balloon, and one nylon hose doughnut. Use a nylon hose strip to tie the doughnut to one of the outer doughnuts on the flying disc. This is your new center doughnut. Tie each of the outer doughnuts to the new center doughnut, just as you did when making the flying disc. Place an uninflated round balloon inside the geode, and then blow it up. When the ball takes shape, tie off the balloon.

GAMING TIP

How to Have a Plan B

One of the most important details that we often overlook is the need to have a Plan B—a backup plan. More games should be planned than are needed, so that there are substitutes ready to use. It is always better to be overprepared than to have played all your games with the night only halfway through. Or too many or too few students show up and you are not able to play the games that you had originally planned.

Occasionally, even well-planned and well-executed games do not work. Don't pretend that everything is going great with the game when it isn't. Students can spot a fake a mile away. If things aren't going well, admit it and switch to good old Plan B. Your kids will appreciate the honesty. Be willing to acknowledge a game that flops (although of course you won't find any of those in this book!) and move on. If something goes wrong or a game never gets off the ground, use the opportunity to make fun of the game. If a game falls flat and the leader is funny about it, kids will still have a good time.

Sometimes a game that is going nowhere may be saved by forming more groups or by modifying in another way (such as increasing the number of runners and chasers or by adding an additional ball into the play). And sometimes it is best to just move on!

OCEAN WAVE

Supplies: chairs

The students sit in chairs about two feet apart in a circle with one student standing in the center. There should be one more chair than there are players seated. The student in the center is trying to sit in the empty seat. However, the empty chair is constantly changing. You call out to the group "Go right," which tells the players that they must keep the chair on their right filled—that is, they continue to move to the right. The students sitting in the chairs keep moving around from chair to chair to prevent the one in the middle from sitting down. You may say to the group "Stop, go left," whereupon they shift directions and must move to the left. If the group is moving to the right, the person who permits the center player to occupy the chair on his right must then take the place of the person in the center. The players do not move until you tell them which way to shift. As the students get up and move from chair to chair, the circle looks like a moving ocean wave.

Game Twist: Have two vacant chairs in the circle and two volunteers in the center of the circle.

ODD OR EVEN

Supplies: beans

Each person is given a dozen beans. Players with any number of beans (1-12) concealed in their hands should go up to other players and say, "Odd or even?" The other player may guess "odd," and since there are three beans in the first player's hand, that second person collects the three beans. If the person had guessed "even," he or she would have had to turn over to the first player the number of beans in question (three in this case).

Game Twist: The players have their hands behind their backs and play a combination of Odd and Even and Fingers Up. When both players bring their hands out with any number of fingers revealed, each partner yells out either odd or even. Count all the fingers, and whoever is right gives the other person one bean.

OVER AND UNDER BALL PASS

Supplies: ball

Divide your group into teams of 10 to 12 students who stand in line facing the same direction. The first person in line in each team passes a ball over his or her head, and the next person in line passes the ball between his or her legs. This procedure continues until the last person gets the ball and runs to the front.

Take it to the next level: Use a foam noodle, foam pipe insulation, or water balloon instead of a ball.

OVER THE LINE

Supplies: bat, softball, cones (or other markers)

Here's a great softball game that has been very popular on Southern California beaches for many years. All that is needed is a bat, softball, at least six people (three on a team), and some way to mark the boundaries of the playing field.

The batter stands at home plate and tries to hit the ball over the line (in the air) in fair territory. The ball is pitched from someone on the team that is at bat, with the pitcher standing 15 or 20 feet from the batter and lobbing the ball up to be hit. The pitcher cannot interfere with the ball after it is hit or the batter is out.

The team members in the field positions themselves in fair territory (anywhere they want). If they catch a hit ball before it hits the ground, the batter is out. Anything that drops into fair territory on the fly is a base hit. A ball hit in fair territory over the heads of all three fielders is a home run.

There are no bases, so no base running. The bases are imaginary. When a person gets a base hit, the next batter comes up and hits. It takes three base hits (not four as in regular softball) before a run is scored, then every base hit after that adds another run. A home run after the first three base hits would score four runs (clearing the bases, plus one bonus run), and it takes three more base hits to start scoring runs again. Other rules include:

- You can play having as many pitches until you get a fair hit, or each batter gets only two pitches to get a hit. If you don't get a hit in two pitches, you are out.
- You can play allowing the person to hit the ball as many times as needed, or any ball hit on the ground in front of the line is an out (unless it's foul on the first pitch).
- Each team gets three outs per inning, as in regular softball.
- The game is played for as many innings as you want.
- Instead of using a softball, you could use a mush ball or volleyball.

How to Put a New Spin on a Classic Game

Modify an old favorite game by making a minor change, and you've got yourself a totally fresh experience. For example, change the ball (play basketball with a volleyball or play football with a teddy bear). Or change the team sizes or team dynamics. For example, play the game once with a group of girls and a group of boys, and the next time have a group of seniors and freshmen and a group of juniors and sophomores. Even adding new music or sounds to an old game can give the game a boost; for instance, buy a buzzer or cowbell for your relay races.

Or try one of these ideas:
- Add a strobe light.
- Add a fog machine.
- Change the rules.
- Change the boundaries.
- Change the object of the game.
- Change the locomotion—the way people move while playing the game. (For example, hopping, holding one hand behind the back, holding someone's hand, crab-walking, and so on.)
- Change the location.
- Change the amount of time to play the game.
- Change the time of day.

GAMING TIP

PAPER SHOOT

Supplies: large clean garbage can (about 3 feet high), paper, duct tape

Set up a garbage can in the middle of the room, and prepare ahead of time several paper batons (rolled up paper wrapped in duct tape) and a lot of wadded-up paper balls.

Have your students form teams of five to eight students. One team lies down around the garbage can with their heads toward the can (on their backs). Each of these players has a paper baton. The opposing team stands around the garbage can behind a line about 10 feet or so away from the can. This line can be a large circle drawn around the can. The opposing team tries to throw the wadded-up paper balls into the can, and the defending team tries to knock the balls away with their batons while lying on their backs. The opposing team gets one or two minutes to try and shoot as much paper into the can as possible.

Game Twist: To make the game a bit more difficult for the throwers, have them sit in chairs while they toss the paper balls.

PASS THE CUPS

Supplies: cups (paper or other kind)

Gather 10 students around a table with a cup in each student's hand (cups are facing down on the table). Everyone says these words together: "We pass the cups

right to left like this. We pass the cups and we never, never miss." As you say this together, students are picking up and placing down each cup from their right hand to their left and their left hand to the person to the left of them. At the same time, they are picking up a cup that is being passed to them. When they receive or pass a cup, they bang it on the table. Every other word in the chant is the one they pick up and pass on. Pick up and pass on the words *pass, cups, to, like, we, the, and, never,* and *miss.* Start off slowly and build up speed until you get into a rhythm on this game. See how fast you can pass the cups!

PAT AND RUB

Supplies: none

Students form a circle with you in the center. Tell the students to rub their stomachs with their right hands while patting their heads with their left hands. When you call, "Change movement!" they must reverse the direction as they pat their stomachs. To make the game even more difficult, you may also call out, "Change hands!" The players must then move their left hand from head to stomach and their right hand from stomach to head without disturbing the pat-and-rub pattern.

Game Twist: Tell the players to grab their left ears with their right hands and stroke their noses with their left hands. At the command of "Change hands!" the same rules apply as in Pat and Rub.

PENNY IN A BALLOON

Supplies: pennies, 11-inch transparent latex balloons (the kind you can see through)

Select balloons that are made for use with helium. They're thicker and last longer than typical party balloons. Most people don't realize that you can put things inside balloons (such as marbles, small candies, Ping-Pong balls, or anything that rolls around or makes noise).

My favorite is a penny, which will roll around the inside of the balloon when the balloon is rotated. By using clear latex balloons, you can watch the penny spin.

Put the penny inside the deflated balloon. If the balloon neck is too thin, insert your fingers on either side of the neck. Stretch the neck and drop the penny in. Then inflate the balloon and tie it off. Warning: As you blow up the balloon, be sure to hold it downward so the penny doesn't roll back into your throat.

After the balloon is inflated, hold the balloon with one hand over the top and begin to rotate your wrist. At first the penny will bounce around inside the balloon. If you keep going, eventually the penny will flip onto its edge and begin rolling around the interior surface. Once it gets going, stop rotating your wrist and hold the balloon with one hand over the top or bottom—the penny will zoom around on its own for up to a minute. Have students try with their own balloon and see how long they can keep it going.

PICK YOUR FRIEND'S NOSE

Supplies: large bedsheet, poster board, or newsprint; scissors; marker

I like the title of this game better than the game itself (although it's a good game). Use a large piece of poster board or newsprint, and draw three stick figure people on it. Cut out the spaces for their noses.

Have students taken turns sticking their noses through the holes. The paper or sheet has to be big enough to hide their bodies. The rest of the students try to see if they can determine whose noses are seen. They'll end up "picking" their friends' noses!

PIZZA BOX FLIP

Supplies: pizza boxes, table, tape

When the pizza party comes to an end and teenagers are just milling around and waiting for their rides home, start a little game. Tape the empty pizza boxes shut, and set up a couple of target tables about 20 feet away from a throw line. Students will toss the pizza boxes like a Frisbee and try to get them onto the table. It's really great if the box lands on the table without hanging over the edges!

PLUNGER HEAD

Supplies: plungers (make sure they're new!), marshmallows, kite string

This game requires two plungers per team. Take one plunger off of the stick, and put it at the end of the other stick, so you end up with one stick with a plunger on each end. Tie a 2-foot section of kite string to the middle of the stick, and on the other end of the kite string tie a marshmallow. Put the plunger on the foreheads of two students. Instruct them to swing the marshmallow around the stick. The object is to see who can get the marshmallow totally wrapped around the stick. Make sure other students get a chance to experience this game as well.

(Game adapted from Jaroy Carpenter, *Get 'Em Pumped*, www.solidrockresources.com)

Take it to the next level: Use a small water balloon instead of a marshmallow.

POOP DECK

Supplies: masking tape (or chalk)

Clearly mark off three equal sections on the floor with tape or chalk. One section is the Poop Deck, one section is the Main Deck, and one section is the Quarter Deck. Begin with everyone standing in the Poop Deck section. Call the name of a deck (even the one that they are standing in) and the students then run to the deck that you have called. The last few people (whatever number you choose) to get to the deck don't continue. If the students are in Poop Deck, for example, and you call, "Poop Deck," any student who crosses the line, jumps the gun, or in any other way (except being pushed) goes off the Poop Deck section, doesn't continue. Call the decks loudly and distinctly. Occasionally point to a different deck than the one you're calling to make it more difficult.

(Game adapted from Wayne Rice and Mike Yaconelli, *Play It!*)

PRINCE OF PARIS

Supplies: none

Have students sit in a circle. Select an "It" who remains in place. Ask all of the players except "It" to number off consecutively. "It" then says, "The Prince of Paris lost his hat. Have you found it, Number 4, sir?" Number 4 jumps to his feet and replies, "Who, sir, I sir?"

"It" remarks, "Yes, sir, you, sir!"

Number 4 says, "No, sir, not I, sir!"

"It" asks, "Well, sir, who then, sir?"

Number 4 says, "Number 7, sir," or any other number within the group. Number 7 must respond in the same manner as 4. If a player fails to answer correctly, he exchanges places with "It," who takes the number of this individual.

PUDDING LEGS

Supplies: snack-size pudding, clean queen-size pantyhose

You'll need several containers of snack-size puddings and several pairs of queen-size pantyhose. Players each pull a pair of pantyhose over their heads so their heads and face are completely covered. Then give each student a small container of pudding that must be eaten as fast as possible through the pantyhose, with the hose serving as a "strainer."

Game Twist: Have teams of two, with one person wearing the pantyhose and the other feeding a partner with a spoon. Also consider playing boys versus girls, with one representative from each coming up front to play the game.

Instead of pudding, give each contestant a bowl of especially runny gelatin in the most seasonal color (green for St. Patrick's Day or red for Valentine's Day). Finally, as an option, pureed baby food can be used instead of pudding.

PULL OFF

Supplies: none

This is where all the boys link up (get in a big pile, hold onto each other, and do whatever is necessary to try to stay linked together). When you say "go," the girls will try to pull them apart. Once a boy is pulled to where he isn't touching any other boy, he's out. Boys can't fight the girls; they can only hang on and try to stay in the pile. The game ends when there are only two boys left. For the obvious reasons, I don't suggest reversing the gender roles on this game.

(Game adapted from Wayne Rice and Mike Yaconelli, *Play It!*)

How to Make Game Formations

The physical formation of a game has a psychological effect on the players—and you can use that insight to your advantage. For instance, a circle formation has a unifying effect on the players by giving them a feeling of belonging and being a part of the group. The circle formation allows players to see who's in the game and helps people get acquainted. Plus, the circle helps players to forget themselves as they participate in activities with the other members of the group.

Games that call for players to assemble, scatter, and then reassemble (like Elephant Stampede on page 61, for instance) minimize self-consciousness by keeping everyone busy. As they move about, players meet each other, and because they're responding to each other, there's a high degree of awareness. When a game leader reassembles the group, the leader usually finds the players in an increasingly open and friendly mood.

GAMING TIP

PUMPKIN GAMES

Supplies: rotting pumpkins

You can purchase leftover rotting pumpkins super cheap in late October or early November. Here are some games you can play:

- Pumpkin bowling
- Pumpkin shot put
- Pumpkin catapult
- Pumpkin soccer

PUZZLED WORDS

Supplies: paper, pens

Write out words and then cut them up into single letters, giving each letter of a given word a number. For example, if one of the words is *battle*, number each letter of the word *battle* with the number 1. So the pieces would look like this: B1, A1, T1, T1, L1, E1.

Give each student one piece of paper with a letter and a number on it. Instruct all the number ones to get together. The teams are to discover what their word is. When their number is called, they should act it out for the group to guess.

Game Twist: Cut up well-known proverbs instead of words.

GAMING TIP

How to Use Word Games

Word puzzles, Mad Libs, and trivia knowledge games are still a hit with teenagers. Years ago such games included questions related to types of plants, types of animals, names of state capitals, names of U.S. presidents, and so on. Today's games include names of movies, actors, sports stars, or celebrities. Two cautions: Make sure you don't overuse word games, and make sure the game you plan doesn't remind your students of school (not that there is anything wrong with school!).

QUESTION GAME

Supplies: none

Have your students form groups of five to eight, and have one person start by asking a question of another student. This can be any question, as long as it's appropriate. The questioned student then asks someone else in the group a different question; this third person then asks another person another question, and so on. The object is to stay active in the game. Participants become inactive by doing one of the following four things:

- Answering a question asked of them.
- Hesitating more than three seconds before coming up with another question.
- Repeating a question asked at any time during the game.
- Asking a question of the person who just asked them a question (this is ignored when there are two students still active).

QUICK POCKETS

Supplies: items found among players

Have your students form teams of four to six people. Once everyone has a team, the group members have to choose a runner. The role of the runner is to bring up the item you call out. This item must be found among the team members. Some examples of items you might call out include: photo I.D., pocket lint, nail file, a strand of hair 10 inches or longer, a hair tie, movie ticket stub, shoelace, sock with a hole, watch, or comb. Have the team members chant the runner's name as he or she brings the item to you.

Take it to the next level: Call out not only an item but also a way that the runner is to make it to the front (crawling, crab-walking, hopping on one foot, or skipping).

RECEIVING LINE

Supplies: none

This game gives everyone a chance to meet everyone else. This game could be used right at the beginning or before you are going to take a break in your meeting. Students line up next to each other in the room. The second person in line moves in front of the first person (face to face), shakes hands, and introduces him- or herself, and then stands on the other side of the first person and becomes the first person in the line. Immediately the third person moves in front of the new second person (face to face) and does the same thing, and so on. This continues until everyone has had a chance to shake hands and introduce themselves.

RHYTHM

Supplies: chair

Everyone in the room numbers off in a circle with Person 1 sitting in the "number 1" chair. (You may want to label this chair so everyone can keep track of it.) Person 1 begins in rhythm by first slapping thighs, clapping hands, then snapping right hand fingers, then snapping left hand fingers in a continuous 1-2-3-4 motion at a moderately slow speed. Everyone joins in the same pattern and keeps in rhythm. The group may speed up after everyone learns how to play. The real action begins when Person 1, on the first snap of the fingers, calls "one" and on the second snap of the fingers, calls somebody else's number. For example, Person 1 goes slap, clap, then says, "One, six" while snapping fingers. Everyone in the group is doing the motions. Then Person 6 goes slap, clap, and says, "Six, ten," and Person 10 slaps, claps, and follows the same, and so on. You may choose to lightheartedly have people move to the end of the numbered progression when they miss, so that everybody moves up one number. In this case, the object is to arrive at the number 1 chair.

Game Twist: Try Symbol Rhythm. Instead of using numbers, each person uses a symbol such as a cough, a whistle, or a head scratch. For example, each person would first do their own and then someone else's symbol (such as slap, clap, cough, scratch head). Or try Animal Sounds Rhythm and substitute animal sounds for numbers.

How to Lead a Game for Special-Needs Students

The physically challenged teenager's need for recreation is as great as that of the less physically challenged student. The key is to select a game in which they can find success and a sense of personal accomplishment, as well as have fun!

What is most important is that the physically challenged student be given the chance to participate in games. Often their need for personal expression and social involvement is so great that they are able to physically engage in games that you might have thought would be literally impossible for them.

The primary difficulty of mentally challenged teens is in grasping complicated skills and ideas and in fully understanding and using verbal communication. Therefore, patience is a prime requisite for you and the other students. Select games that have simple rules, limited strategy, and a minimum of required explanation in order to play. Each game should be explained slowly and clearly, and you should be prepared to repeat instructions, if necessary.

Here are a few ideas for including special-needs teenagers in your game times:

• Have an able-bodied student pair up with a physically challenged young person so they can work together.

• Have the special-needs students be the photographers during the game time.

• Have the special-needs students serve as the referees, judges, or timers.

The important thing is to reach out to these students and make sure they are an important part of the group. (For more information, contact Young Life. They have a terrific ministry to developmentally challenged young people called "The Capernaum Project.")

GAMING TIP

SARDINES

SARDINES

Supplies: none

This is my favorite game to play at night (although it can be played anywhere with a lot of space, indoors or outdoors). The game is similar to but the opposite of the classic game of Hide-and-Seek. In Sardines, one person who is "It" hides, while the rest of the group counts to 100 or until a signal is given. Now the entire group sets out to find the one who is hiding. Each person should look individually, but sometimes it is fun to have small groups of two or three students looking for "It." When a person finds "It," instead of yelling to the rest of the group where the person is or running away from the person who is hiding, the finder hides with "It." Now there are two people hiding in the same place.

When someone else finds the two, there may not be enough room for all three, so the hiding place may be changed an unlimited number of times during the game. As the hiding group gets larger, it becomes more challenging to find places to hide as a group. The last person to find the hiding group (which at this point may be giggling uncontrollably and really has come to resemble sardines in a can) becomes "It" for the next game.

SCATTER BALL

SCATTER BALL

Supplies: a ball that is soft

Establish a playing area about 50 feet square. Have the students scatter about the playing area. Start the game by throwing a soft ball onto the field. Each player then tries to tag the other players with the ball. Any player touched anywhere by the ball while it is on the fly leaves the round. When the ball touches the ground it becomes "dead" and may be picked up and thrown by anyone. The ball is also "dead" after it has hit one player. Have the players no longer playing in the round help recover the ball when it goes out of bounds and toss it back onto the field of play. The game continues until one player is left; then start another round.

SELTZER GAMES

Supplies: Alka-Seltzer tablets (or cheap substitutes), buckets or bowls

The object of this challenge is to see how long students can keep their mouths shut with a fizzing tablet in their mouths, which are full of water. You will want to have buckets or large bowls for students to empty their mouths into. (For added twisted fun, have students stand across from each other so if one explodes, they drench the person across from them!)

Take it to the next level: Have students each put an Alka-Seltzer tablet in their mouth and read a story. Or tie a tablet around each student's neck with a string (like a necklace), and give them all squirt guns (or have them bring their own) to see who remains with the tablet around their neck the longest. This is a "dress for the mess" game.

SERIAL STORY

Supplies: spool of yarn

Pick one of your most imaginative students to start, and give that student a spool of yarn. This student should start a "yarn" of the most ridiculous, elaborate, funny, or weird story—and carry it to a cliffhanger, where the student holds the end of the yarn and tosses the spool of yarn to somebody else in the group. Whoever gets the spool must pick up the "thread" of the story and continue it until throwing the spool to another student. The last student must finish the story.

SEWING UP THE GAPS

Supplies: none

All but two of the students form a single circle, with hands not joined. One of the two players who aren't in the circle is the "chaser," and this person is held back until someone counts to 10. The other of the two (the runner) is allowed to start running in and out through the circle. As this student goes between two people, they sew up the gap by joining hands, and the student runs on and tries to sew up the circle before the chaser can catch him. The runner may run between any two players, but the chaser may not go between players whose hands are joined. When the runner succeeds in sewing up all the gaps or is caught, the chaser becomes the chased and the other player chooses another chaser. The former runner joins the circle.

SHARE AND SHARE ALIKE

Supplies: paper, pens or pencils

Create small groups of four to six students, and give all of the groups five minutes to make a written list of things they all share in common. They should ask each other questions like, "Do you listen to the _____ [name of popular music group]?" or "Do you like fries from _____ better than _____?" "Do you watch _____ [name of TV show]? After time is called, have the groups tally up the number of commonalities. The group with the longest list should be the first to have one student read it aloud.

SHOE KICK

Supplies: players use their own shoes

Have your students each take off one shoe and hang it off the end of their foot. The idea is to see how far students can "kick" their shoes. You'll be surprised to see how many wind up kicking their shoes behind them or straight up into the air!

Game Twist: Create teams and have each person on each team kick one shoe into the middle of the field. On the count of three, the teams all try to put their shoes back on as fast as they can.

SILENT ANIMAL CIRCLE

Supplies: none

Have your students form a circle, and assign each player the name of an animal and a hand motion that represents that animal. Here are a few examples:

- Elephant: Have one arm down with your other arm wrapped around it, holding your nose—there's your trunk!
- Mosquito: Use your left hand to make a peace sign with the inside of your hand facing you. With your right hand, point your index finger forward and place it in the middle of the peace sign in your left hand. Now bring your hands up to your face—you now have a mosquito nose!
- Cow: Put your hand on your stomach with your fingers sticking out like an udder.
- Deer: Point each hand's index finger upward and place your hands on top of your head. Now you've got deer antlers.
- Moose: Open your hands with your fingers spread wide and place your hands on your head with thumbs touching the top of your head. These are your moose antlers!

Let's say that 12 people are playing this game, and everyone is in a circle. Whoever is in the 12 o'clock position of the circle is the elephant, and the elephant is the leader. In the 11 o'clock position is the mosquito; after that you can do the animals in whatever order you like. Here's the key: The animals don't change position. As the students move, they assume the role of the animal in that particular spot.

The elephant starts the game by making the elephant signal, then another animal's signal (such as the cow). The second student (the cow) must then do that animal's (cow's) signal and another animal's signal immediately. A certain rhythm or speed is set by the elephant (by how fast that student does the signals).

The object is to be the elephant. When students make mistakes in this game, they move back to the 1 o'clock position and keep working their way up again.

It goes like this: Let's say that the cow is always in the 10 o'clock position. If the person who is the cow messes up, then he or she goes to the 1 o'clock position to be a different animal, such as a snake. The person who was in the 9 o'clock position is now the cow, and so on down the line. Whenever someone messes up, it is only the people below that person who are affected and have to move up to a new animal. If the elephant messes up, everyone moves because he is the highest position.

(Game adapted from Jonathan McKee's Web site, www.thesource4ym.com)

SNAKE

Supplies: none

Have your students stand in lines in teams of eight to 12. All students should reach their right arms through their own legs and grasp the left hands of the students behind them, and at the same time grasp the right hands of the students in front with their left hands.

On signal, the end player lies down on the ground; all other players walk backward, straddling players as they walk and continuing to hold hands. When all the players are on their backs, the last player to go down gets up and, walking forward, pulls the next player up. This action continues until all players are up without breaking the line.

SNATCH

Supplies: masking tape, handkerchief

Have your students form two teams. Mark two lines on the ground about 30 feet apart, and have each team stand behind its line, facing the other. Then have players number off from right to left.

In the center of the space between the lines, place a handkerchief on the ground. You can also set something like a rock in the center and place the handkerchief on top of it.

Call a number. The players on each side who have that number run out to the center. The one who gets there first snatches up the handkerchief and dashes back to his or her team's line. The players from the other team try to tag this student. This player will be safe and score points for the team if the player reaches the line without being tagged. If the other players succeed in tagging this player, their team receives points.

Very often both runners reach the handkerchief at the same instant. When this happens, each one tries to wait until he or she has a good chance to get a head start before snatching the handkerchief. Each runs in, pretends to grab for the handkerchief, and does everything possible to get the other player a little ways away from the rock.

One thing is important. Don't touch the handkerchief while pretending to grab for it. If touched, even though it is not picked up, then the other player can tag that person and score points.

How to Use Great (Cheap) Resources

If you want inexpensive, cool stuff for playing games, order catalogs from toy stores or online craft and toy companies. These kinds of companies sell things like: furry-headed trolls, fake mustaches, harmonicas, costumes, puppets, inflatable guitars, kazoos, whistles, glow-in-the-dark bouncy balls, Nerf anything, grass hula skirts, pink flamingo yard ornaments, maracas, 3-D glasses, finger toys, noisemakers, pompoms, Slinkys, paddle balls, Frisbees, water guns, boomerangs, yo-yos, Hula-Hoops, crazy wigs, straw hats, plastic sunglasses, basketballs, volleyballs, soccer balls, plastic snakes, rubber chickens, beach balls, kites, silly string, admission tickets, and tons more. These catalogs contain thousands of items!

Also browse toy, craft, and dollar stores. I also go to local swap meets and flea markets. Whenever I enter one of these places, I keep my eyes peeled for stuff I can use in a game. Whenever you're shopping, remind yourself that every aisle is hiding a potential game.

Creative game-planning is not your responsibility alone—surround yourself with other creative people. Your volunteers and student leaders may not want to lead a game, but might be great at helping you create them. Also, there are many Web sites you can use as catalysts for game-planning, such as www.youthministry.com.

GAMING TIP

SOCCER BY THE NUMBERS

Supplies: masking tape, ball

Divide your group into two equal teams. Have each team number off and then line up opposite each other about 30 feet apart (a gym will work fine). Mark a line in front of each team to designate the scoring area. A ball is placed in the middle of the field, and you call a number. The players on each team with that number run to the ball and try to kick it through the other team (across their line). It must go between the other team members' bodies and below their heads (or below the waist) to count as a goal. These team members can catch the ball and toss it back to their own player or kick it back when it comes to them. After a minute or two, you can call a new number. It really gets wild when you call several numbers at once!

Game Twist: Play the game with four teams. The four lines would be laid out as a square. When a number is called, four players (one from each team) run to the center and try to kick the ball through any one of the other three teams.

SOCK TAIL RELAY

Supplies: belts (or ropes), socks, oranges

Make a sock tail for each team (a belt or rope with a sock tied onto the middle of the belt or rope that has an orange in the end of the sock). The first person on each team puts on that belt or rope with the sock hanging down from the student's behind. Another orange is placed on the floor. At the signal, the player must push the orange on the floor to a goal and back with the sock tail. If a student touches it with feet or hands, that person must start over.

(Game adapted from Wayne Rice and Mike Yaconelli, *Play It!*)

SOUND EFFECTS

Supplies: old sheet, pencils, table, watch, index cards, various objects (see ideas below)

Provide a number of items that will make a distinctive sound when dropped on the floor; for example: a pie plate, a shoe, six pieces of silverware, a woman's purse, five pennies, a magazine, a handful of paper clips, a deck of cards, and a basketball. You'll also need a watch. Obtain an old sheet (but not so old that the players can see through it). Suspend the sheet, making sure that it goes down to the floor. Place the items on a table behind the sheet. Appoint an assistant in advance to perform as Chief Dropper behind the sheet and drop the items, one at a time, at 30-second intervals.

Players sit and face the sheet. Distribute the cards and pencils, and ask each player to write the numbers 1 through 10 on the left side of the card. On signal, the Chief Dropper starts dropping the items. The players try to identify each object as it is dropped. They write the names of all objects they can identify to the right of the corresponding number.

After the tenth item is dropped, have the Chief Dropper step from behind the sheet and present the items for the players to compare to what they wrote.

SPARROW FIGHT

Supplies: none

It is best to play this game on a thickly carpeted floor. Have your students crouch down and grab their ankles, remaining in this hunched position throughout the game.

Students hop around holding their ankles and moving their elbows like a bird flaps its wings. The goal is to knock over other players without losing their balance. Like bumper cars, students hop around and bump into each other with their shoulders or behinds. If they're knocked over, they must move out of the playing area. The goal is to stay upright as long as possible (well, actually scrunched down holding their ankles). The play area can be fairly small because movement in the sparrow position is limited.

Even though there's a lot of physical contact, no one should get hurt because everyone's so close to the ground. Also, a chorus of quacks by spectators will liven up the game.

SPELL MY FEET

Supplies: marker

Divide your group into teams of eight to 10 students. Have them take off their socks and shoes. Use the marker to write random letters on the bottom of each person's bare feet. Have everyone in each team sit down in a line. After everyone is ready, call out a word. Each team should spell out the word quickly and correctly. Students must try to stay seated. Use words like water, chicken, and picture, or choose random letters like RSTLNE.

Game Twist: Write individual letters on sticky notes, and put them on students' foreheads or backs. Or write individual letters with a dark-colored marker on either side of both of the students' hands.

SPITTOON

Supplies: water, buckets, Ping-Pong ball, paper cups

Divide your group into teams of four to eight students. Set out paper cups of water for everyone. Each team member should get a mouthful of water, run to the bucket holding the Ping-Pong ball, and spit the water into the bucket. The goal is to float the Ping-Pong ball out of the bucket.

STAND ON THIS

Supplies: blanket (or sheet, carpet, or rug)

Get a piece of material like a blanket that your whole group can stand on. Then have students work together to turn over the blanket without having anyone step off the blanket or touch the floor.

STICK THE TAIL

Supplies: blindfold, stickers, posters of famous people or photocopy machine, paper (or overheard projector and transparency)

Try this new variation of an old birthday party game. Instead of a cartoon drawing of a donkey, use posters of famous people. (Note: You may want to laminate the poster first so it won't get destroyed.) Or create your own picture by photocopying a drawing or piece of clip art onto a sheet of transparency, placing it on an overhead projector, and tracing the picture onto a large sheet of paper taped to the wall. Buy some stickers, and be creative about your choices.

Blindfold your first contestant, have the student turn in a circle a few times, and then nudge the student in the direction of the poster. The goal is to get their stickers closest to the designated target area.

STICKY NOTE CEILING

Supplies: sticky notes

This is best played in a room with a ceiling about eight to 10 feet high. Put sticky notes on the ceiling (or have students do it!). Have students form pairs. On the count of three, have one partner get on the shoulders of the other and attempt to take the sticky notes off the ceiling with his or her mouth. Then have partners switch places.

(Game adapted from Jaroy Carpenter, *Get 'Em Pumped*, www. solidrockresources.com)

SURFER-WAVE-GORILLA

Supplies: none

This game is a lot like the old paper-rock-scissors game (originally an Asian game called Jan Ken Po). You'll say "one, two, three!" and on "three," everybody turns around and instantly assumes one of three poses. Demonstrate these so that everyone knows what to do for each character.

1. Surfer: Act like you are riding on a surfboard, extending your arms and wiggling your hips for balance. Yell "Cowabunga!"

2. Wave: Put both arms up above your head and in the shape of an arch. Yell "Whoosh."

3. Gorilla: Put both arms up and spread out with a fierce look on your face. Growl.

Each of these is superior to one of the others and inferior to another: The surfer defeats the wave, the wave defeats the gorilla, and the gorilla defeats the surfer.

Have everyone in your group pair off and stand back-to-back with their partners. Then say "go," and have partners face each other—each partner in character.

If both partners have chosen the same role, the game is repeated, with new roles chosen. Game continues until the last couple plays. It is best for you to demonstrate this game several times to the group before playing.

Take it to the next level: Try Surfer, Wave, Gorilla, Dragon. Same as above, but the best two out of three wins the match, and the people who win the rounds become the head of the dragon. Meanwhile, the others grab onto their shoulders or waist and follow them wherever they go. The heads of the dragons challenge each other with three more rounds of Surfer, Wave, Gorilla, Dragon. Each dragon team goes into a huddle and decides to be one of three things: a surfer, a wave, or a gorilla. The two teams face each other and advance on signal, each team acting in the manner of the character it has chosen. The dragon that loses the match now latches on behind the winner (think conga line!). This process continues until there are only two long dragons remaining. The final match is an extended three-out-of-five round to determine the fire-breathing champion.

Other variations include: Alien, Human, Laser (laser can beat human; human can beat the alien; alien can beat the laser); and Mongoose, Poisonous Snake, Human (mongoose can beat snake; snake can beat the human; human can beat the mongoose).

TAG GAME VARIATIONS

Supplies: none

• **Sore-Spot Tag.** A student who is tagged and becomes the chaser must hold one hand on the spot touched by the tagger and keep it there as long as he remains the chaser.

• **Toilet Tag.** If a student who is "It" tags you, you must drop to one knee and stick out your right arm. For people to un-tag you, they must sit on your knee and pull your arm down, resembling someone flushing the toilet.

(Game adapted from Wayne Rice and Mike Yaconelli, *Play It Again!*)

• **Triangle Tag.** Have your students form teams of four. Three students hold hands in a triangle, facing each other (one of them is appointed the target). The fourth person is the chaser and should be outside the triangle. The object of the game is for the chaser to tag the target. However, the dynamics of the game are unique: The three players in the triangle all cooperate to protect the target by moving and shifting. The target cannot be tagged on the hands or arms or from across the triangle between the protectors. There can be several triangles and several chasers going at the same time.

• **Slapstick Tag.** This is a great game to play during a retreat or camp experience, or anywhere you and your students will be for a substantial period of time. The game continues during regular activities (over a day's or week's time).

First, write each student's name on a game piece and make sure there are enough pieces for everyone (game pieces could be 2x2-inch cardstock with names written on them). Then give each student a game piece, and tell students that this is the name of the player they must try to "tag" during the time period—or periods—you determine.

Once the students tag the people on their game pieces, the tagger throws away the game piece, and the tagged people are out of the ongoing game. These tagged people give the game pieces they had to the people who just tagged them. Now those left in the game have new people to find and tag. Play until there's one person with a game piece (with his or her name on it).

Consider setting up some guidelines for this game, including:
• Everyone must have their game piece with them at all times.
• There is no running inside buildings.
• Playing in certain areas (bathrooms, offices, chapel, classrooms, and so on) is not allowed.

• **Maze Tag.** A chaser and a runner are selected and the other players stand in rows of sixes or eights, each row at double-arm distance from the next. The width of the row should be such that the group approximates a square. The players extend arms horizontally sideways, and the chaser pursues the runner up and down the passages formed; neither may break through the arms. From time to time you give some selected signal, and the row players make a right face, so that the players are now perpendicular to their former direction. This change is confusing and frustrating to both chaser and runner, but you should time the changes so as to favor the chaser. The chase continues until the runner is tagged; then the runner becomes chaser, the old chaser joins the group, and a new runner is appointed.

If you're looking for Tag immunity options, some ideas include:
• While touching any piece of wood (growing plants are not considered wood)
• While touching a tree, grass, paint, wall, stone, or iron
• While hanging from any support, with both feet off the ground or floor
• While in the squatting position
• While standing on one foot
• While one hand is on the floor

TAKE IT AWAY

Supplies: tissue paper, drinking straws

Divide your group into teams of equal number (about six to eight students sitting in chairs). The first player in each team picks up a piece of tissue paper by sucking through a straw. This student then presents it to the next player (still on the end of a straw), who has to take it away and pass it on in a similar manner.

When the paper reaches the last player, this student must hurry (still carrying it on his straw) to the other end of the line while everyone is moving down to make room for this student. As soon as the last student occupies the first chair, he or she passes on the paper as before. This continues until the original last player occupies the chair he started on and the paper has reached him. If at any time the paper falls to the ground it must be picked up, with the straw, by the person who dropped it.

TAPE HEAD

Supplies: nylon stockings, duct tape, various small objects (see ideas below)

Beforehand, set out an assortment of small, light objects. Possible objects include: small marshmallows, rubber bands, foam cups, inflated balloons, pieces of newspaper, or foam peanut stuffing.

Have your students form teams of four to six, and get a volunteer from each team to be Tape Head. Have the Tape Heads put nylon stockings over their heads (over ears and down to eyebrows, or down over nose but not over mouth). Then wrap their heads with duct tape, sticky side out. The nylon stockings protect the students' hair and skin from the duct tape.

The Tape Heads crawl to an area where the small, light objects are spread out. Tape Heads must lower their heads onto the objects so they stick. Each Tape Head then crawls back to teammates, who remove the objects. This process is repeated for a set period of time as teams try to collect the most objects possible.

Take it to the next level: Have each team stand around its Tape Head, who is seated. On a given signal, team members stick as many of one kind of item as they can on the Tape Head in a designated amount of time. For example, you might say "Shoelaces in 10 seconds," or "Loose change in 11 seconds," or "Foam peanuts in 14 seconds," or "Cotton balls in 7 seconds." Each team attempts to collect the most objects possible on Tape Head.

THREE BUTTONS

THREE BUTTONS

Supplies: 3 buttons (or other small objects) per student

Have your students form teams of four to six, and give each student three buttons, pebbles, or other small objects. At each turn the players have a choice of keeping their right hands empty or putting one or more buttons in them. You'll say to the players, "Hold your hands out," and all the players put their closed right hands out in front. Each player in turn then guesses a number that is *not* the correct total of all the buttons in *all* the players' hands in his team. A player can guess any number between zero and the total number of buttons being used. If there are four players, for example, there will be a total of 12 buttons. After each player has made a guess, all students open their hands and the buttons are counted. Any player who has guessed the correct number drops out, and the game is played until there is only one player.

How to Modify Supplies

Most games may be modified to meet the supplies available. All balls (and many objects) are more or less interchangeable. Lines may be widened, narrowed, lengthened, and shortened. Circles may be made larger or smaller. You can adapt games to almost any situation!

GAMING TIP

THUMBLESS STUNTS

Supplies: adhesive tape, box, wrapping paper, string, oranges

Give your students adhesive tape to tape their thumbs and forefingers together, making the thumbs on both hands useless. Here are some stunts you can ask them to do:

- Give each player a box, some wrapping paper, and piece of string. Each person will try to wrap up the box and tie the string around it.
- Untie the shoelaces of each player. At a signal to start, each player must retie his laces.
- Give players oranges and let them try to peel them.

How to Begin a Game

One of the most popular ways to start a game is by flipping a coin. You can slap the coin on the back of your free hand and, keeping it covered, ask, "Heads or tails?" You'll start with the group that calls the side correctly.

Or a player can hold a coin in one hand, hiding hands behind his or her back. This student can pass the coin to the other hand or keep it in the same hand—the object being to confuse the other group members. This player then brings two clenched hands out in the open, and the others must guess which hand contains the coin. Whoever correctly guesses may begin first.

Another way to determine who begins is to have two group representatives face each other, both with one fist behind their back. On the count of three, they both throw out a number of fingers, calling "Evens!" or "Odds!" The group of the player who guesses correctly may start the game.

TOE FENCING

Supplies: none

Have students take off their shoes, form pairs, and lock hands with their partners. Now partners should try to tap the top of one of their partner's feet with their own feet. In other words, one player tries to step on the other player's foot while their hands are clasped. Of course, since players are also trying to avoid having their feet stepped on, they are all hopping around the floor in a frantic dance.

When a player has had his foot tapped three times, that student is out of the game, and his or her partner pairs up with someone else. The game continues until one person is left (or until the music runs out).

(Game adapted from Wayne Rice and Mike Yaconelli, *Play It!*)

TWISTED KNOTS

Supplies: none

Get your students into teams (about eight to 10 students), and have them stand in a circle facing each other. Tell them to put their arms out in front of each other and to hold hands with people across the circle. They must not hold both hands of the same person or hold a hand of either person beside them. They can't let go of the other person's hands throughout the game. The objective is to work together as a team and untangle the circle without letting go of their hands. In order to untangle the circle, they must go over and under people's arms.

VOLLEYBALL VARIATIONS

Supplies: volleyball, net, and various supplies listed

Here are some ideas to give a new spin to a favorite game:

• Raise the net to 15 feet (no one can spike over this).
• Change the ball to a weather balloon, water balloon, giant pushball, Nerf foam ball, balloons tied together, or Ping-Pong ball.
• Lower the net to four feet above the ground, and have participants sit on their knees.
• Change the number of people who have to hit the ball before it gets over the net (for example, everyone on the team, two boys, or two girls).
• Tie everyone together or have partners hold hands.
• Have players stand on one foot, sit, lie down, stand with backs to the net, or kneel.
• Use a solid cloth for the net so it's impossible to see the other team or the ball until it comes over the net.
• Play in a room lit only with black light.
• Have groups of two or four hold the corners of a beach blanket to throw water balloons over the net.
• Use two balls.
• Play in a racquetball court, using all the walls and ceiling.

WALKING ON WATER

Supplies: two 2x6 boards about 8 feet long, drill, rope

You will need to make two skis from two 2x6 boards. Drill holes in each board, and thread a rope through the holes. Tie a knot on the end under the board. Have students line up on the boards with one foot on one board and the other foot on the other board, all facing the same direction. Have them hold the ropes attached to the boards, one in each hand. Working together with their feet on the boards, students should lift each board and attempt to take a step. Once they get the hang of it, encourage them to move to an object several yards away or move around an object.

Take it to the next level: Use three boards. Half the team puts one foot on one board. The other half of the team has one foot on the other board, and all of them have one foot on the middle board. This is challenging, but it can be done.

WHAT WOULD YOU DO?

Supplies: paper, pens

Prepare slips of paper and number them in pairs, two slips marked 1, two slips marked 2, and so forth. On one of these two slips write, "What would you do if…" and on the other, "I would…"

Distribute one slip of paper and a pen to each student. Students who have slips with "What would you do if…" should complete the sentence by describing a situation. Those whose slips say "I would…" should write what they would do in a situation (unrelated to what anyone else is writing).

Then ask a player holding slip number 1 saying, "What would you do if…" to read the question, and then ask another player holding slip number 1 to read the answer. Since the two people have worked independently, the question and answer are usually not related. For example, the question might be, "What would you do if your Aunt Matilda got seasick?" and the answer, "I would teach the puppy to have better manners."

Game Twist: Write on one piece of paper "Why…" and on the other "Because…"

131

WHERE AM I?

Supplies: none

A student volunteers to leave the room. While the person is out of the room, the others make up a story about where the student is and what the student is supposed to be doing. When the person returns, he or she may ask any question of the group that can be answered by "yes" or "no." The student must guess within five minutes where the group decided he or she was and what the student was doing. If the others had decided that the volunteer who left the room was "Hanging from the chandelier playing a saxophone at the party," the questions and answers might go:

Q. Am I at this party?
A. Yes.

Q. Am I in this room?
A. Yes.

Q. Am I sitting down?
A. No.

And so on…

WHISTLE TALK

Supplies: none

One player "says" something by whistling it. For example, the student might whistle, "It's a nice day," and the others try to discover what he "said." The one who succeeds is next to "whistle talk."

A variation might include getting your students in pairs and having each partner whistle something.

How to Adapt Popular Board Games and TV Shows
Almost any TV or board game can be adapted to fit the needs of your group. Some games that I've adapted for my youth group include *Amazing Race, Family Feud, Who Wants to Be a Millionaire, Fear Factor, Survivor, Pictionary,* and *Gestures.*

WHO'S ON MY BACK?

Supplies: paper, pens or pencils

Have everyone secretly write down the name of a famous person on a small piece of paper. It has to be someone who everyone in the room would know (Jesus, George Washington, a famous singer or actor). After they've written the person's name (making sure no one sees it), students will tape the paper to the back of the person to their left. Students must now go around and ask yes-or-no questions about whose name is on their back. They can only ask each person one question. The goal is to guess the name on their back in a small number of tries.

WILL IT FLOAT?

Supplies: photo (see ideas below), video camera, TV/VCR, body of water (such as lake, pool, or tub)

This game was inspired by David Letterman. Take a photo of an object—an old tricycle for example—then videotape someone dropping the object into a lake or pool. Repeat this for several different items.

Choose some volunteers, and show them the picture of each item one at a time. Have the students guess whether or not the item will float. Then show the footage of the item being dropped into the lake or pool. The goal is to guess correctly as many times as possible. (Note: If the item is not biodegradable, tie fishing line on it to retrieve it.)

ZIP/ZAP/BOOM

Supplies: chairs

Everyone in your group sits in chairs in a circle. Each person must learn the name of the person to his or her left (Zip) and right (Zap). One volunteer stands in the center of the circle and points to someone, saying "Zip" or "Zap." The appointed person must say the correct name of the person in the Zip or Zap position before the person in the center counts to five. If correct, the pointer points again to another person. If the receiver was wrong, that person takes over the position in the center. The center person has a third alternative—to say "Zip, Zap, Boom!" This means that everyone must get up and change seats. The center person tries to grab a seat, making someone else the center person.

How to Hold Game Nights

If you have a game night where you play several games in one evening, I suggest including five different types of games.
1. An athletic game.
2. An intellectual game.
3. A game where kids work together in groups.
4. A boys versus boys game and a girls versus girls game.
5. A game involving food.
(I would offer one caution on playing food games. I am a strong believer in not wasting food. It needs to be eaten, not wasted or tossed around. With millions of people starving in the world, it's inappropriate to use food as a prop that will later be thrown away.)

GAMING TIP

Worst GAMES Ever

Here's a list of the absolute worst game ideas I've ever heard about or observed. They seem almost unbelievable, and it goes without being said that no one should *ever* play any of these games with teenagers. I include these worst games as a shocking reminder that we should always lead games that encourage, inspire, and build community among students.

· Racially offensive games

At different times in history almost every racial group has been singled out or made fun of by a game. How sad that adults would use play to indoctrinate teenagers into the hatred of a few. In selecting and leading games we need to be sensitive to all the racial groups in our community. We also need to be aware of games that use stereotypical phrases and any other subtle forms of racial bias.

· Games whose words have different meanings today

I ran across a very old game called "We Are All So Gay." The word was meant as a synonym for "happy" back then, but obviously it would be interpreted very differently today.

· Games that stereotype the sexes

To illustrate this one, here's an example. In "Boy or Girl," a leader would choose several "victims," an equal number of boys and girls. The leader would explain that everyone is part male and part female. This test was meant to establish what percent of each the person contains. The leader would then have the victims in rotation do the following:

- Light a match
- Drink some water from a glass
- Look directly at the leader
- Look at their fingernails

The leader would then determine if the victim is 25 percent, 50 percent, 75 percent, or 100 percent girl or boy.

That is ridiculous! And, if you're interested, these were the supposed differences: A girl lights a match away from herself; a boy toward himself. A girl looks over the glass while drinking; a boy looks into it. A girl's eyes waver; a boy looks directly at you. A girl extends her hand palms down, fingers away from her; a boy extends it palms up, fingers folded in.

• Games that draw attention to a person's physical appearance

I've read suggestions in several books about dividing students into groups based on the following:

- weight or size ("fat," "thin," "medium")
- level of attractiveness ("ugly," "hot," "indifferent")
- whether they are bowlegged, knock-kneed, or straight-legged
- whether they have hook noses, snub noses, or straight noses

• Humiliating games that make students the target of a joke

There are way too many games that fall into this category, but here are a few examples:

- **Ping-Pong Ball Blow** —The student is blindfolded and told to blow a Ping-Pong ball out of bowl, but the ball is taken out and is replaced with flour.
- **Guess the Weight**— The student ends up sitting on a pan of water or shaving cream.
- **Slander**—A student is sent out of the room, and the group makes negative remarks about the student while he or she is gone. The student is brought back in, and the leader reads the remarks that were made. Appallingly, the student has to guess who made the remarks.

• Games that belittle the loser

This is pretty self-explanatory. I read about an awful game called "Hit the Dud," in which the loser in a game stands facing a wall while the remainder of the group stands behind a throwing line about 50 feet behind the player. At a signal, all students at the line should throw the ball at the "Dud."

· Games that are dangerous

I went over a lot of this already in the Safety Guidelines on page 7, and it's all common sense, right? Well, not for everyone. There is actually a game called "Don't Get Burned," in which students try to tell the most things about themselves while holding lighted matches. And, worse than that, there is a game called "Snap Dragon" where a leader pours alcohol in a pan, lights it with a match, and throws raisins into the burning liquid. "Adventurous" students snatch out raisins as best they can.

Also in this way-too-dangerous category is "Needle in the Haystack," which I found in a book dated—believe it or not—2004. The leader is supposed to hide a bunch of large knitting needles in a big pile of hay, then turn the students loose, telling them to throw the hay up in the air. Students are supposed to bring the needles to the leader as they find them.

One last *very* dangerous game that I'll list is called "Hot Seat." It involves an ordinary wooden stool that has been wired with a six-volt lantern battery and a car coil. Unbelievably, its function is to give the person sitting on the "hot seat" an electric shock that usually sends him (or her) leaping off the seat.

GAME ACTIVITY INDEX

GAME OBJECT INDEX

GAME FORMATION INDEX